The Handy
LONDON
MAP & GUIDE

KT-434-625

CONTENTS

Admission charges

The entrance prices quoted in this guide are for adults only. Where charges apply, there are usually reduced prices available for children, concessions and occasionally for groups. Some places of interest offer free entry to young children when accompanied by an adult.

Opening hours

It should be noted that the opening hours given in this guide may not apply on public holidays and that the *last admission* time is usually earlier than the *closing* time. Please check in advance with the particular establishment.

Star ratings

All monuments, museums and attractions listed in this guide are of some interest, but the most significant sights are classified to provide the reader with an indication of their relative importance for visitors to London. The star ratings are defined as follows:

★★★★★	Exceptional
★★★★	*- worth a journey*
★★★	Very Interesting
★★	*- worth a detour*
★	Interesting

Published by **Bensons MapGuides** (London)
Tel. 020-7724 0040 • Fax 020-7723 0356

Copyright © Fernando Benito & Pedro Benito, 2001.
Edition 8 (2001).

All street maps in this publication are based upon aerial photographs supplied by AEROFILMS LTD., and original field surveys and research by F. Benito and P. Benito.

ESSENTIAL SIGHTS

■ BRITISH MUSEUM ★★★★★   22 A3
The national collections of archaeology, prints and drawings, coins and medals and ethnography. This museum, the greatest and biggest of its kind in the world, was founded in 1753 and occupies a neoclassical building begun in 1823 to the designs of Sir Robert Smirke.

Its incomparable collections of antiquities include treasures such as the Portland Vase, the Rossetta Stone, the Parthenon sculptures (Elgin Marbles) and the Egyptian mummies.

The new **Great Court** is a glass-roofed atrium with exhibition spaces, lecture theatres, shops and restaurants. The **Reading Room** has computer touchscreens allowing access to information about the Museum's huge collections.

To fully enjoy your visit, collect a free map of the museum from the information desk in the Great Court. *Open daily 10am-5.30pm (until 8.30pm Thu and Fri); admission free;* ☎ *020-7636 1555; www.british-museum.ac.uk;* ⊖ *Tottenham Court Road, Russell Square, Holborn.*

■ BUCKINGHAM PALACE ★★★★   37 C1
The principal residence of the sovereign since the accession to the throne of Queen Victoria in 1837. When the Queen is in residence, the Royal Standard is flown from the flagpole. *The State Apartments are open for a few weeks in Aug and Sep daily 9.30am-6pm. Last admission 4.15pm; adult £11.00;* ☎ *020-7321 2233.*

The biggest attraction of the palace is the colourful ceremony of **Changing the Guard**★★★★ which takes place at 11.30am usually daily (alternate days early Aug to Apr), affairs of state and weather permitting. ⊖ *Green Park, St. James's Park, Victoria.*

■ HOUSES OF PARLIAMENT ★★★★   38 B1
A majestic building in the late Gothic style, known officially as the New Palace of Westminster, which stands on the site of the old royal Palace of Westminster (founded in the 11C, rebuilt in the 13C and 14C and burnt down in 1834).

Designed by Sir Charles Barry, assisted in the details by Augustus Pugin, and built between 1837 and 1888, it incorporates the crypt of St. Stephen's Chapel and Westminster Hall (two surviving parts of the medieval palace). The building occupies over 8 acres and, besides the House of Commons and the House of Lords, it contains offices, libraries, dining hall and other rooms. The interior is not open to the public but it is possible to attend the debates when the House is in session; gain access by queuing at St. Stephen's Entrance. ⊖ *Westminster.*

At the north end of the building stands London's most famous landmark: the majestic **Big Ben**★★★, the name usually given to the graceful 320 ft Clock Tower, although it should really only be applied to the bell that strikes the hours and weighs over thirteen and a half tons.

At the southwest corner of the building stands the **Victoria Tower**★ (1860) which houses the archive for parliamentary documents, some of which date back to 1497. At the west side of the building stands **Westminster Hall**★★★ with a splendid **hammerbeam roof**★★★ which is the finest of its kind in the world. Built in the 11C and rebuilt to its present form in the 14C, it has witnessed the most famous state trials in English history. *Not usually open to the public.*

■ NATIONAL GALLERY ★★★★   30 A2
With over 2,000 paintings on exhibition, this is one of the greatest and most important galleries in the world and probably the one that best covers all schools and periods of European painting from the 13C to the beginning of the 20C. Each of the schools is represented by some exceptional works. *Open daily 10am-6pm (Wed until 9pm); admission free;* ☎ *020-7747 2885 www.nationalgallery.org.uk;* ⊖ *Charing Cross.*

■ ST. PAUL'S CATHEDRAL ★★★★   32 A1
Sir Christopher Wren's masterpiece, the seat of the Bishop of London, was built (1675-1710) on the site of the old Gothic cathedral burnt down in the Great Fire of 1666. It is a beautiful Renaissance building dominated by the splendid dome (365 ft high), the largest in the world after St. Peter's in Rome.

The **interior** impresses by its amplitude and for the wealth of its ornamentation. See in particular, the inner face of the great **dome**★★★★; the **monument** to Wellington (in the nave); the **monument** to Nelson (in the south transept); the wrought-iron **gates** by Tijou (Choir) and the **organ case** and beautiful choir **stalls** both carved by Grinling Gibbons and the **crypt**★★★ containing more than 100 tombs including those of Nelson, Wellington and Wren.

CLIMB TO THE DOME: from the south aisle a staircase *(259 steps)* leads to the **Whispering Gallery**, 100 ft above the floor of the cathedral. A further climb *(118 steps)* leads to the external **Stone Gallery** at the base of the dome. From here there are extensive **views**★★★ of London. The last part of the climb, the hardest *(153 steps)*, brings you to the **Golden Gallery** at the foot of the lantern, 295 ft high, which offers impressive **views**★★★ over London.

OPENING HOURS: Open to sightseers 8.30am-4pm Mon-Sat only; adult £5; ☎ *020-7236 4128* ⊖ *St. Paul's, Mansion House.*

■ SCIENCE MUSEUM   *See page 13.*

■ TATE BRITAIN ★★★★   38 A3
The new national gallery of British art showing works from 1500 to the present day. Works by artists from different periods are displayed side by side in a series of themed galleries.

The magnificent Turner Collection, in the **Clore Gallery**, exhibits some of the 282 oil paintings and over 19,000 drawings and watercolours that Turner left to the nation. *Open daily 10am*

5.50pm; admission free; ☎ 020-7887 8000; *www.tate.org.uk;* ⊖ *Pimlico.*

■ TATE MODERN ★★★★   32 A2

Britain's new national gallery of modern art housed in the vast space of the transformed Bankside Power Station. It displays the Tate Collection of international twentieth-century art and features major works by influential artists. Works are grouped in four sections of classic themes: the nude, landscape, still life and history painting. New twenty-first century art is also exhibited. *Open Sun-Thu 10am-6pm, Fri-Sat 10am-10pm; admission free;* ☎ *020-7887 8000; www.tate.org.uk;* ⊖ *Blackfriars, Southwark.*

■ TOWER OF LONDON ★★★★★   33 B2

Imposing fortress by the Thames, which has been a royal residence, a state prison and now-adays is one of London's main tourist attractions, watched over by the famous Yeoman Warders who wear picturesque uniforms designed in the 16C. The origins of the Tower date back to 1078 when William the Conqueror began building its oldest part, the White Tower. The walls and the rest were constructed at later stages.

The most important parts are: the **White Tower**★★★★, which contains a collection of arms and armour and, on the second floor, the **Chapel of St. John**★★, the oldest church in London (1080); the **Crown Jewels**★★★ kept in the Jewel House; the **Medieval Palace**, where King Edward I lived in the 13C; the **site of the scaffold**, where the most noble heads rolled, including those of two of Henry VIII's wives, Anne Boleyn and Catherine Howard; the towers **Beauchamp, Wakefield** and **Bloody**; the **Traitors' Gate** through which the boats with provisions or prisoners once entered.

OPENING HOURS: Mar-Oct, Mon-Sat 9am-6pm and Sun 10am-6pm; Nov-Feb, Tue-Sat 9am-5pm, Sun-Mon 10am-5pm; last admission one hour before closing time; adult £11.30; ☎ *020-7709 0765;* ⊖ *Tower Hill.*

■ VICTORIA AND ALBERT MUSEUM ★★★★   35 D2

The V & A is Britain's National Museum of Art and Design, founded in 1851 by Prince Albert, husband of Queen Victoria.

The museum houses many of the greatest decorative art treasures from around the world. Here you will find the national collections of Sculpture, Ceramics and Glass, Furniture and Woodwork, Textiles and Dress, Silver, Jewellery and Metalwork.

The V & A keeps the world's greatest collection of Constables and a magnificent Dress Collection, which shows the history of European costume and fashion from 1600 right up to the present day. *Open Thu-Tue 10am-5.45pm, Wed 10am-10pm; adult £5, free for under-18s and over-60s (free to all after 4.30pm);* ☎ *020-7942 2000; www.vam.ac.uk;* ⊖ *South Kensington.*

■ WESTMINSTER ABBEY ★★★★★   38 A1

The most important building to visit in London because of its architectural interest and more so because of its long association with British history. It has hosted every coronation from William the Conqueror in 1066 to Elizabeth II in 1953, excepting Edward V and Edward VIII, and is the place where many monarchs are buried. In addition, thousands of eminent men and women are also buried or commemorated here.

As it stands today, the abbey was built in the 13C by Henry III in Gothic style, but has had important additions, such as Henry VII's Chapel in the 16C and the twin towers in the 18C. Of prime interest are: the tomb of the **Unknown Warrior**; the unique **Chapel of Henry VII**★★★; the **Chapel of St. Edward the Confessor**★★, containing the Shrine of the Saint (d.1066); and the **Poets' Corner**★★ in which great poets and writers are buried or commemorated.

OPENING HOURS: Mon-Fri 9.30am-4.45pm (also Wed 6pm-7.45pm), Sat 9.30am-2.45pm; last admission one hour before closing time; adult £6; ☎ *020-7222 7110;* ⊖ *Westminster.*

OTHER PARTS OF THE ABBEY:

1 Great Cloisters ★ These date from the 13C and 14C.

2 Chapter House ★★★ Built in the mid-13C, it is a noble octagonal chamber with a central pier supporting the lofty vault. *Open daily 10am-5.15pm (4pm in winter); adult £2.50 (combined ticket with Abbey Museum);* ☎ *020-7222 5897.*

3 Abbey Museum ★ This museum contains an interesting collection of funeral effigies of monarchs and other illustrious subjects attired with dress of the time. *Open daily 10.30am-4pm; adult £2.50 (combined ticket with Chapter House);* ☎ *020-7222 5897.*

4 Dean's Yard A square with a number of medieval monastic buildings and others. On the lower east side, an archway leads to Westminster School.

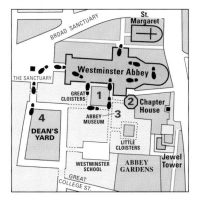

■ ADMIRALTY ARCH   30 A3
A massive curved triumphal arch designed in 1910 as part of a national memorial to Queen Victoria. ✚ *Charing Cross.*

■ ALBERT MEMORIAL ★   35 C1
This monument to Prince Albert (1819-1861), the consort of Queen Victoria, is one of the most original in London, designed by Sir George Gilbert Scott (1872) and recently restored to its original splendour. *Guided tours Sun (please telephone for further details);* ☎ *020-7495 0916;* ✚ *South Kensington.*

■ BARBICAN CENTRE ★★   24 B3
This cultural centre has nine levels (four of which are underground) and includes the splendid **Barbican Hall**, the home of the London Symphony Orchestra; two theatres, the **Barbican Theatre** and **The Pit**, both occupied in winter by the Royal Shakespeare Company; three cinemas, two art galleries, a library, restaurants, cafeterias and a conservatory. *Open Mon-Sat 9am-11pm and Sun 10.30am-11pm;* ✚ *Barbican.*

■ BBC EXPERIENCE   21 C3
A very innovative exhibition where over 75 years of BBC history come to life, allowing one to experience everything from the radio shows to the hi-tech studios of today, from the first flickering black and white images on screen to the latest interactive CD-ROM technology. *Open Mon 11am-6pm, Tues-Sat 10am-6pm, Sun 10am-5.30pm; guided tours every 30 mins, last tour at 4.30pm (Sun at 4pm); adult £7.95;* ☎ *0870-603 0304;* ✚ *Oxford Circus, Gt. Portland Street.*

■ BEDFORD SQUARE ★   22 A3
Built at the end of the 18C, this is one of the most interesting squares in London and has survived with its Georgian houses quite unspoiled. ✚ *Tottenham Court Road.*

■ BELGRAVE SQUARE ★   36 B1
The most majestic square to be seen in Belgravia, boasting on each side an exceptionally impressive range of buildings with houses on a palatial scale. ✚ *Hyde Park Corner.*

■ BERKELEY SQUARE ★   29 C2
This was one of the most aristocratic and elegant squares in London and still retains its beautiful gardens with enormous plane trees, planted about 1790, and some fine old houses on the west side. ✚ *Green Park.*

■ BIG BEN ★★★   38 B1
See HOUSES OF PARLIAMENT, page 2.

■ BRITISH AIRWAYS LONDON EYE   30 B3
See LONDON EYE, page 5.

■ CANARY WHARF TOWER   44 A1
Officially known as *One Canada Square*, this 800 ft high landmark is Britain's tallest building.

■ CENOTAPH   30 B3
National memorial (1920) commemorating all the members of the British and allied forces who gave their lives in the two world wars. ✚ *Westminster.*

■ CHINATOWN ★   30 A2
Filled with a great number of restaurants, the lively Chinese quarter of London centres on Gerrard Street, with its exotic street furniture. ✚ *Piccadilly Circus, Leicester Square.*

■ CITY, THE
The City of London (usually referred to as "The City") occupies the area roughly equivalent to Norman London: about one square mile. The City is governed by a corporation presided by the annually-elected Lord Mayor, 24 other Aldermen and 132 Common Councilmen. The City, in which less than 6,000 people live and where more than 200,000 work, is one of the main financial centres of the world. It has its own police organisation, the City of London Police.

■ CLEOPATRA'S NEEDLE   30 B2
The 68 ft high rose-pink granite obelisk, made in Heliopolis in about 1475 B.C., was given to Britain in 1819 and erected at this site in 1878. ✚ *Embankment.*

■ COVENT GARDEN ★★★   30 B2
In the centre of the square, designed by Inigo Jones in 1631, the market buildings that exist today were built in 1828-31, and housed the principal market for fruit and vegetables in London until 1974. After the market moved out, the buildings were refurbished and are now occupied by shops, restaurants, cafés and pubs, and the whole place has developed into a colourful meeting-point, especially for the young. ✚ *Covent Garden.*

■ CUTTY SARK ★   44 A3
The last of the great tea clippers, launched in 1869, and the fastest ship of its time when it beat the world record in 1871 by sailing from China to London in 107 days. Exhibits illustrate its history and it houses a collection of ships' figureheads. *Open daily 10am-5pm; adult £3.50;* ☎ *020-8858 3445;* DLR *Cutty Sark,* ⇌ *Greenwich.*

■ DOWNING STREET   30 A3
This modest street is famous because No. 10 is the official residence of the Prime Minister. ✚ *Westminster.*

■ DRAKE'S GOLDEN HINDE ★   32 B2
A full size replica of the 16C warship in which Sir Francis Drake circumnavigated the world (1577-80). Launched in 1973, this galleon has sailed over 100,000 miles - many more than the original. *Usually open daily, please telephone for details; adult £2.50;* ☎ *020-7403 0123;* ✚ *London Bridge.*

■ FORTNUM AND MASON ★★   29 D2
This famous department store was founded in 1707 (on the site of the present building) by Messrs. Fortnum and Mason whose effigies appear every hour as the clock above the front door chimes. ✚ *Piccadilly Circus, Green Park.*

■ **GABRIEL'S WHARF** 31 D2

A pleasant enclave of design studios, restaurants and shops. *The shops are open Tue-Sun 11am-6pm;* ✚ *Waterloo.*

■ **GEORGE INN** ★ 32 B3

London's only remaining galleried coaching house. The present building dates from 1676 and originally occupied three sides of the courtyard. It is mentioned in Dickens' *Little Dorrit.* ✚ *London Bridge.*

■ **GRAY'S INN** ★ 23 C3

One of the four Inns of Court within which tranquil surroundings lawyers have worked since the 14C. In the **hall** (1560, rebuilt 1951), Shakespeare's *The Comedy of Errors* was first staged in 1594. ✚ *Chancery Lane.*

■ **GROSVENOR SQUARE** ★ 28 B2

A large and elegant square bordered on the west side by the US Embassy. ✚ *Bond Street.*

■ **GUILDHALL** ★★★ 32 B1

The seat of the Corporation that has governed the City since the first Mayor was installed here in 1189. The foundation of the present Guildhall was begun around 1411, from which remains the medieval wall of the Great Hall, the porch and the crypt. The majestic **Great Hall** is used for municipal and public meetings, banquets and ceremonies. The **Art Gallery** exhibits some of the City's extensive collection. *Guildhall is open 10am-5pm (May-Sep daily, Oct-Apr Mon-Sat); admission free. The Art Gallery is open Mon-Sat 10am-5.30pm, Sun noon-4.30pm; adult £2.50, free for under-17s, free to all daily after 3.30pm and all day Fri;* ☎ *020-7332 3700;* ✚ *Bank, Moorgate, St. Paul's.*

■ **HARRODS** ★★★ 36 A1

The largest and most renowned of London stores, Harrods began as a simple grocery shop in 1849 and now stocks all things luxurious. The present building of terracotta brick dates from 1905 and covers five acres. ✚ *Knightsbridge.*

■ **HAY'S GALLERIA** ★ 33 C3

Once the River Thames's most famous wharf, now a pleasant venue comprising shops, restaurants, cafés and a craft market under a spectacular glass and steel roof. ✚ *London Bridge.*

■ **HORSE GUARDS** ★ 30 A3

This building (18C) provides the backdrop for the theatre of daily pageantry. On the Whitehall side, two mounted troopers are posted daily from 10am to 4pm (guard changes hourly). The colourful ceremony of **Changing the Guard**★ takes place Mon-Sat at 11am and Sun at 10am; the dismounted inspection occurs daily at 4pm. ✚ *Charing Cross, Westminster.*

■ **JEWEL TOWER** ★ 38 B1

This 14C building is the only remaining domestic part of the medieval Palace of Westminster and once housed the King's valuables. *Open daily Apr-Sep 10am-6pm, Oct-Mar 10am-4pm; adult £1.50;* ☎ *020-7222 2219;* ✚ *Westminster.*

■ **LEICESTER SQUARE** ★★ 30 A2

Laid out in the 17C, this pedestrianised square is the undoubted focus of London's nightlife. Located on its south side one finds the official **Half-Price Ticket Booth**, where theatre tickets for same day performances are sold at half-price *(open Mon-Sat noon-6.30pm, Sun noon-3pm).*

■ **LIBERTY** ★ 29 D1

This famous store boasts, on its north side, an interesting mock Tudor façade which was constructed in 1924 using timber from two Royal Navy ships. ✚ *Oxford Circus.*

■ **LINCOLN'S INN** ★★ 31 C1

One of the four Inns of Court founded in the 14C. The most interesting parts are: the charming **New Square** surrounded on three sides by 17C buildings now occupied mainly by solicitors; the **Chapel** (1620-23) raised on vaulted arches; **The Old Hall** which dates back to 1491 and the **Old Buildings** dating mainly from the 16C. *Open Mon-Fri;* ✚ *Chancery Lane.*

■ **LLOYD'S** ★ 33 C1

The world's leading insurance market. Originating in the 1680's, Lloyd's is a society of underwriters who accept insurance risks for their personal profit or loss. The unusual building which it occupies was opened in 1986. *Not open to the public.* ✚ *Bank, Monument.*

■ **LONDON AQUARIUM** 30 B3

One of Europe's largest displays of global aquatic life featuring thousands of living specimens. Built on three levels within historic County Hall, it has vast tanks which allow visitors to get a close look at the fascinating inhabitants of the various natural environments recreated within. *Open daily 10am-6pm; adult £8.75;* ☎ *020-7967 8000;* ✚ *Westminster, Waterloo.*

■ **LONDON DUNGEON** 33 C3

Set in dark vaults below some railway arches, this horrifying exhibition uses special effects to illustrate English medieval torture, execution, disease and witchcraft. A visit includes the dramatic *Great Fire of London*, the *Jack the Ripper Experience* and *Judgement Day* boatride. *Open daily Apr-Oct 10am-5.30pm (until 8pm in summer), Nov-Mar 10.30am-5pm; adult £10.95;* ☎ *020-7403 7221;* ✚ *London Bridge.*

■ **LONDON EYE** ★★★ 30 B3

This highly popular observation wheel is 450 ft tall and provides a superb bird's-eye **view** of the capital's other famous landmarks. With 32 fully enclosed capsules, each accommodating up to 25 people, it operates on a continuous rotation taking around 30 minutes to complete a full 360 degrees. *Open daily 10am-7pm (until 10pm in summer); adult £9/£9.50 (advance booking is strongly recommended);* ☎ *0870-5000 600;* ✚ *Westminster, Waterloo.*

PLACES OF GENERAL INTEREST

■ LONDON PLANETARIUM   20 B3
Using commentary, music and special visual effects visitors are guided through our solar system, galaxies and beyond. *Shows are every 30 minutes from 12.30pm Mon-Fri and 10.30am Sat-Sun, last show at 5pm; adult £7;* ☎ *0870-400 3000;* ✪ *Baker Street.*

■ LONDON ZOO ★★★   20 B1
This is the world's oldest zoo (founded 1826) and keeps one of its most representative collections of animals. *Open daily 10am-5.30pm (until 4pm in winter); adult £10;* ☎ *020-7722 3333;* ✪ *Baker Street (then 274 bus) or Camden Town (then 274 bus or on foot).*

■ MARBLE ARCH   28 A1
Designed by John Nash in 1828, inspired by the Arch of Constantine in Rome, it was placed outside Buckingham Palace and moved in 1851 to its present site, previously known as Tyburn, where public executions were carried out in the six hundred years up to 1783. ✪ *Marble Arch.*

■ MAYFAIR   29 C2
The elegant district denoting the area bounded by Oxford Street, Regent Street, Piccadilly and Park Lane. A fair held each May from 1688 until the mid-18C gave its name to the area, which was mainly developed in the first half of the 18C. It remains a residential district dotted with luxury hotels, restaurants, some embassies, private art galleries, offices and elegant shops.

■ MILLENNIUM BRIDGE   32 A2
The newest bridge to span the Thames is an impressive walkway linking St. Paul's Cathedral to the north of the river and Tate Modern on the south bank. *Closed indefinitely for structural works.* ✪ *Blackfriars.*

■ MILLENNIUM DOME   44 B1
A vast structure, the largest of its kind in the world, which was built as the venue for the *Millennium Experience* during 2000 and to provide a centrepiece for Britain's millennium celebrations. The future of the Dome and its site still remained undecided at the time of publishing. *Not open to the public;* ✪ *North Greenwich.*

■ MONUMENT, THE ★   33 C2
Colossal Doric column surmounted by a flaming urn designed by Sir Christopher Wren and erected in 1681-87. It commemorates the Great Fire of London, which started on 2 Sep 1666 at a baker's in nearby Pudding Lane some 202 ft away from the column which itself is 202 ft high. A spiralling climb of 311 steps leads to a platform that affords panoramic **views*** of the metropolis. *Open daily 10am-5.40pm; adult £1.50;* ☎ *020-7626 2717;* ✪ *Monument.*

■ NELSON'S COLUMN ★   30 A2
See TRAFALGAR SQUARE, page 8.

■ OLD BAILEY   32 A1
It is the principal court for crimes committed in London. Built in 1903-7 on the site of the famous Newgate Prison (demolished in 1902), in front of which public executions used to take place from 1783 to 1868. *The public is admitted when the courts are sitting, Mon-Fri 10.30am-1pm and 2-4pm; admission free;* ✪ *St. Paul's.*

■ OLD OPERATING THEATRE   33 C3
The operating theatre of St. Thomas's Hospital from 1821 to 1862 (discovered and restored in 1956), which was used by Florence Nightingale for her School of Nursing from 1860. *Open daily 10.30am-5pm; adult £3.50;* ☎ *020-7955 4791;* ✪ *London Bridge.*

■ OLD ROYAL OBSERVATORY ★★   44 B3
Established by Charles II in 1675 primarily for navigational research and since 1884 it has been the home of Greenwich Mean Time which divides the East and the West. The zero meridian of longitude passes through here, and millions of visitors have been photographed with one foot on either side of the line. It houses Britain's largest refracting telescope and a unique collection of historic timepieces and astronomical instruments. *Open daily 10am-5pm; adult £6, free for under-17s and over-60s;* ☎ *020-8858 4422;* ⇌ *Greenwich, Maze Hill,* DLR *Cutty Sark,* 🚢 *Greenwich Pier.*

■ PICCADILLY CIRCUS ★★★   29 D2
Flanked by huge neon advertisements, this world-famous crossroads is always busy with crowds of people seeking out the diverse entertainments on offer in the West End. It is adorned by a fountain topped by the famous statue known as **Eros** (the Greek god of Love) which has become a symbol of London and a popular rendezvous. In fact, rather than Eros, the statue was intended to portray the Angel of Christian Charity. ✪ *Piccadilly Circus.*

■ ROCK CIRCUS   40 F2
An exhibition depicting the history of rock music since the 1950's. *Open Mon-Tue 11am-5.30pm, Wed-Sun 10am-5.30pm; adult £8.25;* ☎ *020-7734 7203;* ✪ *Piccadilly Circus.*

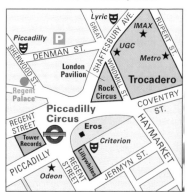

PLACES OF GENERAL INTEREST

■ ROSE THEATRE EXHIBITION   32 A2
This audiovisual presentation takes place on the archaeological site of the Rose. Built in 1587, this was the first theatre on Bankside. *Open daily 10am-6pm in summer, noon-5pm in winter; adult £4;* ☎ *020-7593 0026;* ✛ *Mansion House.*

■ ROYAL ALBERT HALL ★   35 C1
Built (1867-71) in the form of an oval amphitheatre, 273 ft across and 238 ft wide, with an upper frieze around the wall illustrating the triumphs of Arts and Sciences. The hall has a capacity of 5,000 and stages many events, including the famous *Proms* concerts. ✛ *South Kensington.*

■ ROYAL COURTS OF JUSTICE ★   31 C1
The principal courts in the country for hearing civil cases (The High Court of Justice), and for criminal and civil appeals (The Court of Appeal) occupy an impressive Gothic building (1882). *When the courts sit (Oct-Jul) the public is admitted to the galleries, Mon-Fri, 10.30am-1pm and 2-4pm; admission free;* ✛ *Temple.*

■ ROYAL EXCHANGE ★   33 C1
First built in 1565-67 as a meeting place for international commerce, it was made "Royal" by Elizabeth I in 1570. The present classical building was opened by Queen Victoria in 1844, and was used for trading until 1939. ✛ *Bank.*

■ ROYAL FESTIVAL HALL ★   31 C3
One of London's most important concert halls which can accommodate 2,300 for ballet and approximately 3,100 for recitals. The spacious foyers *(open daily 10am-10.30pm)* offer bars, cafeterias, a restaurant, a bookshop and an almost daily programme of live music and frequent art exhibitions. ✛ *Embankment, Waterloo.*

■ ROYAL MEWS ★   37 C1
This is where the Queen's horses and carriages can be seen. These include the Gold State Coach which was built in 1762 and has been used at every coronation since then. *Open all year Mon-Thu noon-4pm, in summer open from 10.30am (please note that all dates and times are subject to alteration); adult £4.60;* ☎ *020-7799 2331 (recorded message);* ✛ *Victoria.*

■ ROYAL NAVAL COLLEGE, OLD ★★ 44 B3
This occupies the site of the royal palace where Henry VIII, Mary I and Elizabeth I were all born. It is an impressive baroque ensemble that was designed mainly by Christopher Wren in 1696 as a hospital for disabled seamen, similar to Chelsea Royal Hospital. From 1873 it became a college for naval officers and continued as such until recently. See the **Painted Hall** with murals by James Thornhill and the beautiful **Chapel**. *Open Mon-Sat 10am-5pm, Sun 12.30-5pm; adult £3, free for under-16s (free to all after 3.30pm Mon-Sat, and all day Sun);* ☎ *0800-389 3341;* **DLR** *Cutty Sark,* ⇌ *Greenwich.*

■ ROYAL OPERA HOUSE ★   30 B1
The London home of international opera and ballet. The present theatre, the third on this site, was built in 1856-8 by E. M. Barry and has recently undergone a major refurbishment. The graceful **Floral Hall** is open to the public Mon-Sat 10am-3.30pm. There are regular backstage guided tours (please telephone to obtain details). ☎ *020-7304 4000;* ✛ *Covent Garden.*

■ ST. KATHARINE DOCKS ★★   33 D2
These once busy docks have been converted into a successful commercial and leisure complex, with visiting yachts, Thames barges and other sailing crafts, adding the atmosphere of a coastal holiday village. ✛ *Tower Hill.*

■ SHAKESPEARE'S GLOBE   32 A2
THEATRE & EXHIBITION ★★
The original Globe, burnt down in 1613, has been rebuilt as part of an educational, cultural and entertainment complex. *Open daily (please telephone for opening times); adult £5 (exhibition only) or £7.50 (including tour of the theatre);* ☎ *020-7902 1500;* ✛ *Mansion House.*

■ SHEPHERD MARKET   29 C3
A charming village-like quarter formed by narrow streets and alleys with shops, pubs, restaurants and cafés that invite one to a pleasant stop. The popular May Fair that gave its name to the district used to be held here. ✛ *Green Park.*

■ SOHO   29 D1
This famous district is bordered by Oxford Street, Charing Cross Road, Leicester Square, Piccadilly Circus and Regent Street. It is composed of a labyrinth of small streets, mostly from the 17C and 18C, with its main road, **Shaftesbury Avenue**, built at the end of the 19C and known for its theatres (Shaftesbury, Apollo, Gielgud, Lyric, Palace and Queen's). Since the 17C Soho has always been a refuge for a cosmopolitan population and nowadays it is a gastronomic centre, where the most important of the world's cuisines are represented. The area is also renowned for its numerous strip clubs and sex shops.

■ SPEAKERS' CORNER   28 A2
An open space just inside Hyde Park, where orators, some brilliant, some uninspired, gather on Sundays to deliver their speeches on political, religious and other issues, providing a free and picturesque diversion. ✛ *Marble Arch.*

■ STAPLE INN ★   23 C3
From the 15C to 1884, this was one of London's nine Inns of Chancery, where law students spent their first year. The unique **façade★**, made up of half-timbered 17C houses (restored), gives an idea of how the City looked before the Great Fire of 1666. ✛ *Chancery Lane.*

■ TELECOM TOWER   21 D3
This famous London landmark is a part of the nation's telecommunications system. On completion in 1965, it was the tallest structure in central London (620 ft).

PLACES OF GENERAL INTEREST

■ TEMPLE, THE ★★★   31 D1
A vast enclosure occupied until 1312 by the military order of the Knights Templars (founded in 1119 in Jerusalem). This enclave of Georgian buildings and gardens, amongst which lawyers have their chambers, is an oasis of peacefulness and tranquillity. It houses the **Middle Temple** and the **Inner Temple**, two of the Four Inns of Court, legal societies which have the exclusive right of admitting persons to practice at the English bar. **⊖** *Temple.*

IN AND AROUND THE TEMPLE:

1 The George This fine timbered inn dates from 1723 when it was opened as one of the fashionable coffee houses.

2 Twinings The tea shop, with a golden lion and two Chinamen above the door, opened in 1706 as Tom's Coffee House.

3 Child & Co. (Now part of the Royal Bank of Scotland). Presumed to be the oldest bank in London, it has occupied the present site (No. 1 Fleet St.) since 1673 (rebuilt in 1879), and is the original of Tellson's Bank in Dickens' *A Tale of Two Cities.*

4 Temple Bar Located in the middle of the road, this monument from 1880 marks the boundary of the City of Westminster and the City of London.

5 Middle Temple Hall ★ In this magnificent hall Shakespeare's *Twelfth Night* was first performed on 2nd February 1602.

6 Temple Church ★ This fine and interesting church, consists of a round nave, completed in 1185, based on the Church of the Holy Sepulchre in Jerusalem and a rectangular Gothic style chancel added in 1220-40. *Open Wed-Sun.*

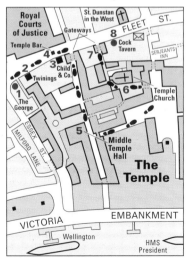

7 Inner Temple Gateway (1610-11), a beautiful half-timbered building which contains a fine 17C room on the first floor: **Prince Henry's Room** *(open Mon-Sat 11am-2pm).*

8 Cock Tavern One of the most famous taverns in the City and the oldest in Fleet Street it was frequented by Pepys, Dickens and Tennyson.

■ TEMPLE OF MITHRAS   32 B1
The remains of a Roman Temple dedicated to the god Mithras. All sculptures that were uncovered here are now in the Museum of London. **⊖** *Bank, Mansion House.*

■ TOWER BRIDGE ★★★   33 D3
Opened in 1894, this world-famous landmark is easily recognised by the twin Gothic towers linked near the top by two fully-glazed walkways 139 ft above water level. An audiovisual exhibition entitled *The Tower Bridge Experience* brings this distinctive bridge's history to life. Visitors can enjoy splendid **views** of the Thames from the walkways as well as entry to the original engine rooms and a mock bascule chamber where the bridge-lifting system is explained. *Open daily Apr-Oct 10am-6.30pm, Nov-Mar 9.30am-6pm, last admission 75 minutes before closing time; adult £6.25;* ☎ *020-7403 3761;* **⊖** *Tower Hill.*

■ TRAFALGAR SQUARE ★★★   30 A2
The most famous square in London, named in commemoration of Nelson's victory over the fleets of France and Spain at Cape Trafalgar along the Spanish coast in 1805. It is a monumental ensemble ornated with statues, fountains and the 170 ft high **Nelson's Column★**. This monument to Lord Nelson is made of granite and surmounted by the statue of the Admiral (erected in 1843). The pedestal at the base is adorned with four bronze reliefs cast from captured French guns. The four colossal lions were added in 1867. **⊖** *Charing Cross.*

■ TROCADERO   30 A2
A large entertainment complex with shops, places to eat, three cinemas, and the latest hi-tech arcade attractions; **⊖** *Piccadilly Circus.*

■ VINOPOLIS - CITY OF WINE   32 B2
An exhibition and dining complex dedicated to the world of wine where visitors can experience a multi-media tour and take part in wine tastings. *Open daily 11am-6pm (Mon until 9pm, Sat until 8pm), last entry 2 hours before closing; adult £11.50;* ☎ *0870-4444 777;* **⊖** *London Bridge.*

■ WELLINGTON ARCH   28 B3
Designed by Decimus Burton, this arch was built in 1826 to commemorate Wellington's victory over Napoleon and offers fine **views** of London's skyline from its balconies. *Open Wed-Sun 10am-4pm (until 6pm Apr-Sep); adult £2.50;* ☎ *020-7930 2726;* **⊖** *Hyde Park Corner.*

■ WESTMINSTER HALL ★★★   38 B1
See HOUSES OF PARLIAMENT, page 2.

■ **APSLEY HOUSE ★★**   28 B3
See WELLINGTON MUSEUM, page 13.

■ **BANQUETING HOUSE ★★**   30 B3
The only important building to survive from the great Palace of Whitehall which was the sovereign's metropolitan residence from 1530 until it was burnt down in 1698. This masterpiece by Inigo Jones was completed in 1622 and has a spacious and well proportioned **Banqueting Hall** which was enriched in 1635 with Rubens' splendid **ceiling paintings★★★**. *Open Mon-Sat 10am-5pm (except when closed for ceremonies); adult £3.90; ☎ 020-7930 4179; ✛ Embankment, Westminster.*

■ **DICKENS HOUSE ★**   23 C2
Home of Charles Dickens from 1837 to 1839 where he completed *The Pickwick Papers* and wrote *Oliver Twist* and *Nicholas Nickleby*. *Open Mon-Sat 10am-5pm; adult £4; ☎ 020-7405 2127; ✛ Russell Square.*

■ **DR. JOHNSON'S HOUSE**   31 D1
Typical late 17C house where Dr. Samuel Johnson lived (1749-1759) while compiling his famous dictionary. *Open Mon-Sat 11am-5.30pm (5pm in winter); adult £4; ☎ 020-7353 3745; ✛ Chancery Lane, Blackfriars.*

■ **KENSINGTON PALACE ★★★**   26 B3
Queen Victoria lived in this modest palace from her birth until her accession to the throne in 1837 and it was the home of Diana, Princess of Wales. Highlights of a visit include the **Royal Ceremonial Dress Collection** and the beautifully restored King's Gallery which displays a collection of magnificent Old Masters. *Open daily Mar-Oct 10am-5pm, Nov-Feb 10am-4pm; adult £8.80; ☎ 020-7937 9561; ✛ Queensway, High Street Kensington.*

■ **MANSION HOUSE ★**   32 B1
Completed in 1752, the official residence of the Lord Mayor of London is a classical building with a Corinthian portico. ✛ *Bank.*

■ **QUEEN'S HOUSE ★★**   44 B3
Elegant Palladian villa designed by Inigo Jones (1616) and completed by 1638 for Charles I's queen Henrietta Maria, who called it her "house of delights". Recently restored to its former splendour, its galleries will exhibit works from the National Maritime Museum's rich art collection. *Open from 18th May 2001 daily 10am-5pm; adult £1, free to under-17s and over-60s; ☎ 020-8312 6565; DLR Cutty Sark, ⇌ Greenwich.*

■ **ROYAL HOSPITAL, CHELSEA ★★** 36 B3
Designed by Christopher Wren, this home for veteran and disabled soldiers, founded in 1682 by Charles II, was inspired by Louis XIV's *Hôtel des Invalides* in Paris. The pensioners, over 400 of them today, wear their blue or scarlet uniforms dating back to the Duke of Marlborough's time.

In the central part of the building are the **Chapel** and the panelled **Great Hall** (dining hall) where

the Duke of Wellington lay in state in 1852. *Open Mon-Sat 10am-noon and 2-4pm, Sun 2-4pm; admission free; ✛ Sloane Square.*

■ **ST. JAMES'S PALACE ★**   29 D3
Built by Henry VIII in 1532, this mansion became the sovereign's official residence in London after the Whitehall Palace fire in 1698 and until Queen Victoria moved to Buckingham Palace in 1837. In fact foreign ambassadors are still accredited to "the Court of St. James's". *Not open to the public; ✛ Green Park.*

AROUND THE PALACE:

1 Lancaster House A beautiful mansion with a very splendid interior where Queen Victoria often visited her friend, the Duchess of Sutherland. *Not open to the public.*

2 Clarence House The London residence of Queen Elizabeth the Queen Mother.

3 Picturesque **Gatehouse** (16C) with octagonal towers and its original linenfold-panelled doors.

4 Queen's Chapel Designed by Inigo Jones it was England's first classical church (1623-7).

5 Friary Court Overlooking this court is the balcony from which the Heralds made the official proclamation of a new sovereign.

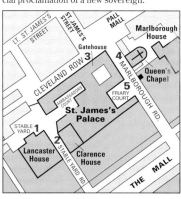

■ **SOMERSET HOUSE ★**   31 C2
A majestic building of 1777-86 designed in classical style by Sir William Chambers, with an impressive frontage to the Thames. The restored expansive **Courtyard** and the **River Terrace** are open to the public, the former being also a venue for events and performances. The building also houses the **Courtauld Gallery★★★**, **Gilbert Collection★★** and **Hermitage Rooms** *(see pages 11-12). Admission free to Courtyard and Terrace; ☎ 020-7845 4600; ✛ Temple.*

■ **SPENCER HOUSE ★**   29 D3
The London residence of the Spencer family. *Open Sun (except during Aug and Jan); all tours are guided and run at regular intervals from 10.30am until 4.45pm (last tour); adult £6; ☎ 020-7499 8620; ✛ Green Park.*

CHURCHES & CATHEDRALS

■ **ALL HALLOWS-BY-THE-TOWER** ★ 33 D2
A church dating back to the 7C and rebuilt several times. The church and crypt are well worth visiting, note especially the beautiful carved font cover and an Anglo-Saxon arch (7C). *Open Mon-Fri 9.30am-5.30pm, Sat-Sun 10am-5pm;* ☎ *020-7481 2928;* ✆ *Tower Hill.*

■ **BROMPTON ORATORY** ★ 35 D1
A Roman Catholic church in the Italian baroque style, consecrated in 1884. The interior, notable for its sumptuous decoration, for the beauty of its design and for its proportions, contains works of art brought from Italy. *Open daily 6.30am-8pm;* ✆ *South Kensington.*

■ **ST. BARTHOLOMEW THE GREAT** ★ 24 A3
This is the oldest parish church in London and one of the most interesting. It belonged to an Augustinian priory founded in 1123 by Rahere, a courtier of Henry I. The 12C choir and the 13C transept constitute the present church which is a notable example of the Romanesque style in its oldest parts. *Open Mon-Fri 8.30am-5pm (4pm in winter), Sat 10.30am-1.30pm, Sun 2-6pm;* ✆ *Barbican.*

■ **ST. BRIDE'S** ★ 31 D1
Built in 1703, this is often nicknamed "the wedding cake church" because of the shape of its **steeple**★, Wren's tallest (226 ft) and perhaps most beautiful. A baker, Mr. Rich, made a fortune making cakes resembling it. In the crypt there is an illustrated record of the growth of the church and its community over a period of nearly two thousand years, set amid the remains of a Roman building and seven churches. *Open daily 9am-4.45pm (Sat until 4.30pm);* ☎ *020-7427 0133;* ✆ *Blackfriars.*

■ **ST. CLEMENT DANES** ★ 31 C1
The central church of the Royal Air Force presents a beautiful steeple added by James Gibbs in 1719, and in the harmonious interior, embedded in the floor, are more than 800 reproductions of the badges of the squadrons and units of the RAF and the Commonwealth. As the famous "Oranges and Lemons" Church, the bells ring merrily at 9am, noon, 3 and 6pm. *Open Mon-Fri 8.30am-4.30pm, Sat 9am-3.30pm and Sun 9am-12.30pm;* ✆ *Temple.*

■ **ST. ETHELDREDA'S** ★ 23 D3
A gothic building of 1290 with a crypt of 1251. This church situated in a private cul-de-sac lined by 18C houses, is the only surviving vestige of the Bishop of Ely's mansion. *Open daily 8am-6pm;* ✆ *Chancery Lane, Farringdon.*

■ **ST. GILES CRIPPLEGATE** ★ 24 B3
A church with 900 years of history, rebuilt in 1545-50 and restored in 1959 after bombs had destroyed the interior in 1940. The poet John Milton is buried in this church (see engraved floor stone close to the pulpit), and Oliver Cromwell was married here in 1620. *Open Mon-Fri 11am-4pm, Sat 9am-noon and Sun 8am-noon;* ✆ *Barbican, Moorgate, St. Paul's.*

■ **ST. HELEN BISHOPSGATE** ★ 33 C1
Known as "the Westminster Abbey of the City" because of the number and interest of its monuments. *Open Mon-Fri 9am-5pm; entrance via church office (south side);* ☎ *020-7283 2231;* ✆ *Bank, Aldgate, Liverpool Street.*

■ **ST. JAMES, PICCADILLY** ★ 29 D2
One of only two Wren churches outside the City, with a spacious and beautiful interior. *Open daily 8am-6.30pm;* ✆ *Piccadilly Circus.*

■ **ST. MARGARET'S** ★ 38 A1
The church of the House of Commons since 1614. The present church, the third on this site, was consecrated in 1523. The **East Window** is unique, made to commemorate the marriage in 1502 of Catherine of Aragon to Prince Arthur, elder brother of Henry VIII. *Usually open for visitors Mon-Fri 9.30am-3.45pm, Sat 9.30am-1.45pm, Sun 2pm-4.30pm;* ☎ *020-7654 4840.*

■ **ST. MARTIN-IN-THE-FIELDS** ★ 30 B2
The present church, the masterpiece of James Gibbs (1722-6) replaced one erected as a royal parish church for Henry VIII in 1544. It is a beautiful example of baroque architecture, featuring an elegant spire and portico. It is a popular lunchtime and evening concert venue. The crypt contains a café, bookshop and brass-rubbing centre. *Open for sightseers Mon-Sat 9am-6pm;* ☎ *020-7766 1100;* ✆ *Charing Cross.*

■ **ST. MARY-LE-BOW** ★ 32 B1
This famous church, built by Christopher Wren (1670-80), replaced the 11C church, which was destroyed in the Great Fire of 1666 except for the Norman **crypt**, built on arches (or bows) of stone, which still survives. The **steeple**★, 217 ft high, is among Wren's finest achievements and houses the famous **Bow Bells** within which sound true Londoners, or "Cockneys", are said to be born. *Open Mon-Thu 7am-6pm, Fri 7am-4pm;* ✆ *St. Paul's, Bank.*

■ **ST. PAUL, COVENT GARDEN** ★ 30 B2
Known as the Actors' Church, it was built by Inigo Jones in 1631-3 and rebuilt after a fire in 1798. Overlooking the square is the great Tuscan portico, the only surviving part of Jones's Church. Beautiful interior with memorials to Noel Coward, Charlie Chaplin, Vivien Leigh and many other actors. *Open Mon-Fri 8.30am-4.30pm;* ☎ *020-7836 5221;* ✆ *Covent Garden.*

■ **ST. PAUL'S CATHEDRAL** *See page 2.*

■ **ST. STEPHEN WALBROOK** ★ 32 B1
This Wren masterpiece has a simple exterior that contrasts with its sumptuous and perfectly proportioned interior. The beautiful **dome**★ may have served as a model for St. Paul's Cathedral. *Open Mon-Fri 10am-4pm (Fri until 3pm);* ☎ *020-7283 4444;* ✆ *Bank, Cannon Street.*

■ **SOUTHWARK CATHEDRAL** ★★★ 32 B3
The Cathedral church of the diocese of Southwark is one of the oldest and most beautiful Gothic churches in London after Westminster Abbey. Its majestic interior contains countless interesting monuments, such as the memorial to William Shakespeare, whose brother Edmund is buried here. John Harvard, the founder of Harvard University, was baptized in the church (1607) and the **Harvard Chapel** is dedicated to his memory. *Open daily 8.30am-6pm;* ☎ 020-7367 6712; ⊖ *London Bridge.*

■ **TEMPLE CHURCH** ★ 31 D1
See TEMPLE, THE; page 8.

■ **WESLEY'S CHAPEL AND HOUSE** 25 C2
The Chapel has been the mother church of Methodism since 1778 when it was opened by the founder John Wesley, who lived in the adjacent house and is buried in the graveyard behind the Chapel. *House, Chapel and crypt museum are open Mon-Sat 10am-4pm; adult £4, (admission free Sun noon-2pm);* ☎ 020-7253 2262; ⊖ *Old Street.*

■ **WESTMINSTER CATHEDRAL** ★★ 37 D2
This is the largest and most important Roman Catholic church in Great Britain and is the seat of the Archbishop of Westminster. Built in 1895-1903, it is an imposing structure in an early Christian Byzantine style presenting an original exterior with alternate bands of red brick and Portland stone. The unfinished interior, which gives the impression of vastness and fine proportions, is ornamented by fine marbles and modern mosaics. *Open daily 7am-7pm.*
Ascending the 273 ft high campanile by lift, one can enjoy an extensive **view**★ over West London. *Open Apr-Oct daily 9am-5pm, Nov-Mar Thu-Sun 9am-5pm; adult £2;* ☎ 020-7798 9055; ⊖ *Victoria.*

■ **BANK OF ENGLAND MUSEUM** ★ 32 B1
This interesting museum uses material from the Bank's collections to tell the history of the Bank since its foundation by Royal Charter in 1694. It also includes an interactive video display explaining the role of the Bank today. *Open all year Mon-Fri 10am-5pm; admission free;* ☎ 020-7601 5545; ⊖ *Bank.*

■ **BANKSIDE GALLERY** 32 A2
Home of the Royal Watercolour Society and the Royal Society of Painter-Printmakers. *Open during exhibitions Tue 10am-8pm, Wed-Fri 10am-5pm, Sat and Sun 1-5pm; adult £3.50;* ☎ 020-7928 7521; ⊖ *Blackfriars.*

■ **BRAMAH TEA & COFFEE MUS.** 33 D3
This museum illustrates the history of tea and coffee since their arrival in this country through a colourful collection of pictures, silver, ceramics and tea and coffee-making artefacts. *Open daily 10am-6pm; adult £4;* ☎ 020-7378 0222; ⊖ *Tower Hill, London Bridge.*

■ **BRITISH LIBRARY**
  EXHIBITION GALLERIES ★★ 22 A1
There are three galleries open to the public of which the most important is the **Treasures Gallery** which permanently displays some 200 of the Library's most famous items including *Magna Carta*, the *Lindisfarne Gospels*, the *Gutenberg Bible* and the *First Folio Shakespeare*. *Open Mon-Fri 9.30am-6pm (Tue until 8pm), Sat 9.30am-5pm and Sun 11am-5pm; admission free;* ☎ 020-7412 7332; ⊖ *King's Cross St. Pancras, Euston.*

■ **BRITISH MUSEUM** *See page 2.*

■ **CABINET WAR ROOMS** ★★ 38 A1
The underground emergency accommodation where Winston Churchill, the War Cabinet and the Chiefs of Staff of Britain's armed forces met whenever London was under attack during the Second World War. Visitors can view 21 of the rooms, including the Cabinet Room, the Map Room and the Prime Minister's room. *Open daily Apr-Sep 9.30am-6pm, Oct-Mar 10am-6pm; adult £5.40, free for under-16s;* ☎ 020-7930 6961; ⊖ *Westminster.*

■ **CLINK PRISON MUSEUM** 32 B2
On the site of the original Clink prison, this exhibition traces its history and displays restraining and torture devices. The prison, known as the Clink since the 15C, was owned by the Bishops of Winchester until it was destroyed in 1780. *Open daily 10am-6pm; adult £4;* ☎ 020-7378 1558; ⊖ *London Bridge.*

■ **CLOCK MUSEUM** 32 B1
Housed in the same building as the famous Guildhall Library, this small museum displays an interesting collection of old clocks and watches from the last five centuries. *Closed for refurbishment May-Dec 2001; normally open Mon-Fri 9.30am-4.30pm;* ⊖ *Bank, St. Paul's.*

■ **COURTAULD GALLERY** ★★★ 31 C2
This gallery displays a superb assembly of private collections including the outstanding Impressionist and Post-Impressionist paintings bequeathed by *Samuel Courtauld*, as well as Renaissance, Baroque and twentieth-century works of art. *Open Mon-Sat 10am-6pm, Sun noon-6pm; adult £4, free to under-18s, free to all Mon 10am-2pm;* ☎ 020-7848 2526; ⊖ *Temple, Covent Garden.*

■ **DALI UNIVERSE** 30 B3
A significant collection of Salvador Dalí's

MUSEUMS & GALLERIES

surrealist paintings, sculptures and furniture displayed in a series of themed areas. *Open daily 10am-5.30pm; adult £7;* ☎ *020-7620 2420;* ✪ *Westminster, Waterloo.*

■ **DESIGN MUSEUM** 33 D3
This museum is devoted to design and its effect on our lives. *Open Mon-Fri 11.30am-6pm, Sat-Sun 10.30am-6pm; adult £5.50;* ☎ *020-7403 6933;* ✪ *Tower Hill, London Bridge.*

■ **FLORENCE NIGHTINGALE MUS.** 39 C1
This museum illustrates the work of Florence Nightingale to improve the standards of hospitals and nursing. *Open Mon-Fri 10am-5pm, Sat-Sun 11.30am-4.30pm; adult £4.80;* ☎ *020-7620 0374;* ✪ *Waterloo, Westminster.*

■ **GEFFRYE MUSEUM** 25 D1
Set in charming Georgian Almhouses, built round three sides of an open court c.1715, this museum contains a fine collection of furniture and decorative art from Elizabethan times to the 1950's. *Open Tue-Sat 10am-5pm, Sun noon-5pm; admission free;* ☎ *020-7739 9893;* ✪ *Liverpool Street (then by 149 or 242 bus).*

■ **GILBERT COLLECTION** ★★ 31 C2
This newly-opened museum comprises some 800 outstanding works of art including European silver, gold snuff boxes and Italian mosaics. *Open Mon-Sat 10am-6pm, Sun noon-6pm; adult £4, free for under-18s, free to all Mon 10am-2pm;* ☎ *020-7420 9400;* ✪ *Temple.*

■ **GUARDS MUSEUM** 37 D1
Dedicated to the history of the five Foot Guards regiments (Grenadiers, Coldstreams, Scots, Irish and Welsh) which extends over more than 350 years. *Open daily (except Christmas period) 10am-4pm; adult £2, free for under-16s;* ☎ *020-7414 3430;* ✪ *St. James's Park.*

■ **HAYWARD GALLERY** 31 C3
Temporary exhibitions of painting and sculpture. *Open daily 10am-6pm (Tue and Wed until 8pm); adult £8, free for under-16s;* ☎ *020-7960 4242;* ✪ *Waterloo, Embankment.*

■ **HERMITAGE ROOMS** 31 C2
Exhibitions from the rich collections of the State Hermitage Museum of St. Petersburg in Russia. *Open Mon-Sat 10am-6pm, Sun noon-6pm; adult £6;* ☎ *020-7845 4630;* ✪ *Temple.*

■ **HMS BELFAST** ★ 33 C2
The last surviving Royal Navy big gun ship, this cruiser was launched in 1938, and is now a floating museum. *Open daily Mar-Oct, 10am-6pm; Nov-Feb, 10am-5pm; adult £5.40, free for under-16s;* ☎ *020-7940 6300;* ✪ *London Bridge.*

■ **ICA (Institute of Contemporary Arts)** 30 A3
Includes an art gallery, a cinema and a theatre. *Art gallery open daily noon-7.30pm;* ☎ *020-7930 3647;* ✪ *Charing Cross, Piccadilly Circus.*

■ **IMPERIAL WAR MUSEUM** ★★★ 39 D2
This museum illustrates all aspects relating to

the two world wars and other military operations involving the armed forces of Britain and the Commonwealth since 1914. Most notable amongst the exhibits are the walk-through *Trench Experience,* the dramatic *Blitz Experience* and the newly-opened *Holocaust Exhibition. Open daily 10am-6pm; adult £5.50, free for under-16s and over-60s (free to all after 4.30pm);* ☎ *020-7416 5000;* ✪ *Lambeth North.*

■ **LONDON'S TRANSPORT MUS.** ★★ 30 B2
This museum tells the story of travel, people and the growth of London itself through a superb collection of transport memorabilia and original vehicles covering nearly 200 years. There is fun for all with exciting *hands-on* exhibits, videos and *touch-screen* displays. *Open daily 10am-6pm (Fri from 11am); adult £5.95, free for under-16s;* ☎ *020-7379 6344;* ✪ *Covent Garden.*

■ **MADAME TUSSAUD'S** ★★★ 20 B3
The famous waxworks exhibition, one of London's most popular attractions, has existed since 1802 and on its present site since 1884. Life-size wax models of famous and infamous world figures, past and present, are displayed in themed areas. *Open from 10am Mon-Fri (9am/9.30am peak periods), and 9.30am Sat-Sun (9am peak periods), last admission at 5.30pm; adult £12;* ☎ *020-7935 6861;* ✪ *Baker Street.*

■ **MUSEUM OF GARDEN HISTORY** 38 B2
This museum is housed in the redundant church of St. Mary-at-Lambeth, with its churchyard converted into a 17C garden with plants of the kind brought to England by John Tradescant and his son. These 17C royal gardeners are buried in the churchyard next to Admiral Bligh (of *Mutiny on the Bounty* fame). *Open Feb-mid Dec daily 10.30am-5pm; voluntary admission fee;* ☎ *020-7401 8865;* ✪ *Westminster, Lambeth North.*

■ **MUSEUM OF LONDON** ★★★ 24 A3
This museum illustrates the history of London and its people from prehistoric to modern times. The story of London is traced in open galleries arranged in chronological order. See the splendid Lord Mayor's Coach (1757) - used once a year for the Lord Mayor's Show. *Open Mon-Sat 10am-5.50pm and Sun noon-5.50pm; adult £5 (ticket valid for one year), free for under-17s, free to all after 4.30pm;* ☎ *020-7600 3699;* ✪ *St. Paul's, Barbican, Moorgate.*

■ **NATIONAL ARMY MUSEUM** ★★ 36 A3
This museum illustrates the history of the armies of Britain, from the raising of the Yeomen of the Guard right up to the present day. *Open daily 10am-5.30pm; admission free;* ☎ *020-7730 0717;* ✪ *Sloane Square.*

■ **NATIONAL GALLERY** *See page 2.*

■ **NATIONAL MARITIME MUS.** ★★★ 44 B3
This recently-modernised museum is the largest of its kind and is dedicated to Britain's seafaring heritage from Tudor times to the present day.

12

Twenty galleries display some of the finest items in its collection covering many aspects of ships, seafaring and marine affairs, in historic buildings which were formerly a school for the children of seamen. The main hall is covered by a huge glass canopy. *Open daily 10am-5pm (last admission 4.30pm); adult £7.50, free for under-17s and over-60s; ☎ 020-8312 6565 (recorded message);* **DLR** *Cutty Sark,* ⇌ *Greenwich.*

■ **NATIONAL PORTRAIT GALLERY ★★★** 30 A2
Displays portraits of the most eminent persons in British history from the age of the Tudors to the present day. The collection, founded in 1856, now comprises more than 10,000 portraits of which only about a third is on view. *Open daily 10am-6pm (Thu and Fri until 9pm); admission free; ☎ 020-7306 0055; www.npg.org.uk;* ⊖ *Charing Cross, Leicester Square.*

■ **NATURAL HISTORY MUS. ★★★★** 35 C2
This museum contains the national collection of fossil and living animals and plants, minerals, rocks, gemstones and meteorites. It is one of London's most popular museums, especially with children who enjoy the *"Creepy-crawlies"* section, the earthquake simulator and the fascinating dinosaur exhibits. *Open Mon-Sat 10am-5.50pm and Sun 11am-5.50pm; adult £9, free for under-17s and over-60s (free to all Mon-Fri after 4.30pm, Sat and Sun after 5pm); ☎ 020-7942 5000;* ⊖ *South Kensington.*

■ **QUEEN'S GALLERY ★★** 37 C1
Presents temporary exhibitions of paintings, drawings and other works of art from the royal collections. *Closed for refurbishment until 2002; ☎ 020-7321 2233;* ⊖ *Victoria, St. James's Park.*

■ **ROYAL ACADEMY OF ARTS ★★★** 29 D2
Housed within Burlington House, an 18C grandiose mansion, the Royal Academy was founded in 1768 with the aim of fomenting the arts in the country. It is internationally renowned for its remarkable loan exhibitions from all around the world. The **Summer Exhibition** (June-August), held regularly from 1769, consists of paintings, drawings, sculptures and architectural models by living artists. *Open daily 10am-6pm (Fri until 10pm); admission fee varies depending on the exhibition; ☎ 020-7300 8000; www.royalacademy.org.uk;* ⊖ *Piccadilly Circus, Green Park.*

■ **SCIENCE MUSEUM ★★★★** 35 C1
The largest of its kind in the world, it houses over 15,000 different exhibits, covering almost every imaginable sector of science, technology, industry and medicine. Its contemporary collections include over 2,000 interactive exhibits through which visitors can explore and discover science and technology for themselves.
The newly-opened **Wellcome Wing** contains a suite of continually updated exhibitions. Also housed here is a 450-seat *IMAX* cinema, showing

2D and 3D science films, and *Virtual Voyages*, a motion simulator ride with a martian theme. *Open daily 10am-6pm; adult £7.95, free for under-17s and over-60s, free to all after 4.30pm (an extra charge applies for all visitors to IMAX and the Virtual Voyages ride); ☎ 020-7942 4000; www.sciencemuseum.org.uk;* ⊖ *South Kensington.*

■ **SERPENTINE GALLERY** 27 C3
Holds temporary exhibitions of modern and contemporary art. *Open during exhibitions daily 10am-6pm; admission free; ☎ 020-7402 6075;* ⊖ *Lancaster Gate.*

■ **SIR JOHN SOANE'S MUSEUM ★★** 31 C1
This museum contains the works of art and antiquities assembled together by the famous architect Sir John Soane (d. 1837) in his own house which he left to the nation with the instruction that nothing should be altered in any way. The interesting collection includes mainly paintings, antiquities, architectural drawings, books, sculptures and furniture. *Open Tue-Sat 10am-5pm; admission free; ☎ 020-7405 2107;* ⊖ *Holborn.*

■ **TATE BRITAIN** *See page 2.*

■ **TATE MODERN** *See page 3.*

■ **THEATRE MUSEUM** 30 B1
Housed in part of the old Flower Market, this museum contains an exhibition illustrating major developments, events and personalities from throughout the performing arts. *Open Tue-Sun 10am-6pm; adult £4.50, free for under-17s and over-60s; ☎ 020-7943 4700;* ⊖ *Covent Garden.*

■ **VICTORIA & ALBERT MUS.** *See page 3.*

■ **WALLACE COLLECTION ★★★** 28 B1
Situated on the north side of the beautiful 18C Manchester Square, this museum is one of London's most elegant and original. It is especially rich in 17C and 18C French art, and contains paintings, sculptures, furniture, porcelain, European and Oriental arms and armours and other objets d'art. *Open Mon-Sat 10am-5pm, Sun 2-5pm; admission free; ☎ 020-7935 0687;* ⊖ *Bond Street.*

■ **WELLINGTON MUSEUM ★★** 28 B3
This occupies the first floor and part of the ground floor of **Apsley House** which was the residence of the first Duke of Wellington from 1817 until his death in 1852. The interior has been restored to its former splendour and contains the works of art collected by the victor of Waterloo and his descendants. *Open all year Tue-Sun 11am-5pm; adult £4.50, free for under-18s and over-60s; ☎ 020-7499 5676;* ⊖ *Hyde Park Corner.*

■ **WHITECHAPEL ART GALL.** Outside 33 D1
Modern and contemporary art exhibitions often of great interest. *Open during exhibitions Tue-Sun 11am-5pm (Wed until 8pm); admission normally free; ☎ 020-7522 7888;* ⊖ *Aldgate East.*

SHOPPING

Main Shopping Areas

■ **BOND STREET** ★★★   29 C2
This comprises two parts: *Old Bond Street*, built c.1686, and *New Bond Street*, c.1720. It is flanked by elegant shops specialising in all things luxurious including respected names such as: *Asprey & Garrard*, for gold, silver and jewellery; *Burberry*, Britain's best-known raincoat brand; and *Sotheby's*, the famous art auctioneers.

■ **CARNABY STREET**   29 D1
World-famous in the sixties as the centre of London's fashion scene, this area is enjoying a revival with the presence of a number of shops selling alternative fashion.

■ **COVENT GARDEN** ★★★   30 B1/2
A lively, cosmopolitan shopping district with markets, boutiques, specialist shops and an abundance of cafés, bars and restaurants. Its focal point is the *Piazza* and the former vegetable market.

■ **JERMYN STREET**   29 D2
Well known for its shirtmakers but two particular shops should not be missed: **Paxton & Whitfield** at No. 93 selling a variety of cheeses since it was founded in 1740; secondly, **Floris** the perfumers at No. 89 since 1730.

■ **KENSINGTON HIGH STREET**   34 A1
A popular shopping area offering a good mixture of department stores and a great selection of trendy clothes shops and boutiques.

■ **KING'S ROAD** ★   36 A3
This 1960's legend, the backbone of Chelsea, has developed into a very popular shopping street. The notable department store *Peter Jones* is at the junction with Sloane Square.

■ **KNIGHTSBRIDGE** ★★★   36 A1
This is a very exclusive area that includes Beauchamp Place and parts of Knightsbridge, Sloane Street and Brompton Road. Goods of the highest quality are offered in fine stores such as *Harrods* and *Harvey Nichols*.

■ **OXFORD STREET** ★★★   28 B1-29 D1
London's most popular shopping street, particularly the section stretching from Marble Arch to Oxford Circus, with department stores such as: *Selfridges*, London's second largest store with an impressive quantity and variety of household and fashion goods; *John Lewis*, with seven floors of merchandise for the home and family; the principal branch of *Marks & Spencer*, with clothes, accessories and homeware; *Debenhams*, with five floors of well-stocked departments; and also *House of Fraser* (formerly *D H Evans*), selling a wide range of quality goods on its seven floors.

■ **PICCADILLY** ★★   29 D2
One of London's most imposing streets with luxury hotels and elegant shops. Here one finds the department store *Fortnum & Mason* with its renowned food hall and the beautiful *Princes Arcade, Piccadilly Arcade* and **Burlington Arcade**★★, a covered passageway built in 1819, with attractive shop windows that are synonymous with elegance and refinement.

■ **REGENT STREET** ★★★   29 D1/2
Laid out at the beginning of the 19C by John Nash, it maintains an air of distinction and is world-known for the elegance and high quality of its shops, such as: *Liberty*, a department store especially famous for its printed fabrics; *Aquascutum*, a world-famous high quality fashion store; *Dickins & Jones*, a department store with five floors of high quality ladies' fashions; *Austin Reed*, a fashion store with four floors of quality menswear; and *Jaeger*, with its exclusively designed English clothes. Also to be found here is *Hamleys*, the internationally-known toy shop.

Markets

The following is a selection of the most popular street markets in the capital:

■ **BERWICK STREET**   29 D1
A picturesque market dating back to the 18C, mainly fruit and vegetables, which also extends into Rupert Street *(Mon-Sat)*.

■ **CAMDEN MARKETS** ★   See map below
Camden's markets have expanded swiftly since opening in 1974 and now extend from Camden Town Underground station to Chalk Farm Road. **Camden Lock Market**, where it all began, is one of the best known and busiest markets in London for crafts, antiques, clothes, accessories and bric-a-brac, *open daily 10am-6pm, best days Sat and Sun*; **Stables Market** sells antiques, curios, collectables, clothing and more, *open Sat and Sun from 10am*; **Camden Market** for clothes mostly (new and secondhand), *open Thu-Sun from 10am*; **Camden Canal Market** sells bric-a-brac, clothes and more, *open Sat and Sun from 10am*.

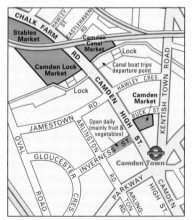

■ **CAMDEN PASSAGE**   Outside 23 D1
A market featuring antiques, furniture, bric-a-brac, old games, prints, jewellery and other collectables. *Open Wed 10am-2pm and Sat 9am-3.30pm;* ✪ *Angel.*

■ **JUBILEE MARKET**   30 B2
A covered market held for antiques (Mon), general goods and bric-a-brac (Tue-Fri) and crafts (weekends). *Open daily 9am-6pm.*

■ **LEADENHALL MARKET**   33 C1
A retail market housed in a Victorian building with elaborate arcades (1881), selling mainly meat, game and provisions. *Open Mon-Fri.*

■ **LEATHER LANE**   23 D3
A busy lunchtime market with plenty of rag trade. *Open Mon-Fri 10.30am-2.30pm.*

■ **PETTICOAT LANE** ★   25 D3
Famous street market crowded and full of character, selling clothes, hardware, jewellery and other goods. *Open Sun 9am-2pm in Middlesex Street and adjacent.*

■ **PORTOBELLO ROAD** ★   Outside 26 A1/2
Famous for the great cosmopolitan atmosphere of its Saturday market, antiques predominate but there are also clothes, silver, chinaware and other collectables. *Open Sat 8am-6pm.* From Mon-Fri there is a general market. ✪ *Ladbroke Grove, Notting Hill Gate.*

Specialist Shopping

■ **CHARING CROSS ROAD**   30 A1
A book-lover's paradise, most of the leading bookstores are to be found here along with a variety of antique, secondhand and specialist bookshops.

■ **HATTON GARDEN**   23 D3
This street is the country's centre for diamonds, gold and silver jewellery.

■ **LONDON SILVER VAULTS**   31 C1
Shops housed in underground vaults with a vast quantity of antique and modern silverware.

■ **TOTTENHAM COURT ROAD**   21 D2/3
A popular street for hi-fi, radio, video and electrical equipment. It is also known for home furnishings.

PARKS & GARDENS

■ **CHELSEA PHYSIC**   Outside 36 A3
GARDEN ★
Botanical garden founded in 1673 by the Society of Apothecaries of London containing more than 5,000 species of plants. *Open Apr-Oct, Wed noon-5pm, Sun 2-6pm; adult £4;* ☎ *020-7352 5646;* ✪ *Sloane Square.*

■ **GREEN PARK**   29 C3
Some 53 acres made a royal park by Charles II.

■ **GREENWICH PARK** ★★   44 B3
The oldest enclosed royal park and the only one east of central London. Within the 183 acres one finds several historic buildings, most notably the **Old Royal Observatory** (see page 6).

■ **HYDE PARK** ★★★   28 A3
& KENSINGTON GARDENS ★★   26 B2
Of the parks in central London, Hyde Park is the most popular and, together with Kensington Gardens, covers an area of 635 acres forming the largest continuous space in London where one can forget for a few hours that this is the centre of a big city. On the lake, called the **Serpentine** in Hyde Park and **Long Water** within Kensington Gardens, it is possible to row and swim in the summer. **Rotten Row**, on the south side, is a famous sandy track reserved for horse riding. The **Serpentine Gallery** (*see page 13*), in Kensington Gardens, holds exhibitions of contemporary art.

■ **REGENT'S PARK** ★★★★   20 A1
With an area of 487 acres, this is the largest and one of the most beautiful parks in central London. It was laid out from 1812 onwards by John Nash for the Prince Regent, along with Regent Street and Portland Place, as part of a "royal mile" connecting the park with the Prince's palace, Carlton House (demolished in 1829), in The Mall. It is enclosed on three sides by classical **terraces**★★, designed by Nash and his disciple Decimus Burton. Each of these terraces has an imposing façade in the style now known as Regency.
Inside the park lies the beautiful 22 acre boating lake and, in the centre, **Queen Mary's Gardens**★★, considered the most beautiful public grounds in London, with one of the nation's best rose gardens. On the north side of these gardens lies the **Open Air Theatre** which was founded in 1932 and opens from June to August, usually featuring plays by Shakespeare, musicals, concerts and children's theatre.

■ **ROYAL BOTANIC**   Outside the map
GARDENS (Kew Gardens) ★★★★
One of the world's finest botanic gardens. *Open daily 9.30am and closing time varies according to the season; adult £5;* ☎ *020-8940 1171;* ✪ *Kew Gardens.*

■ **ST. JAMES'S PARK** ★★★   38 A1
This 93 acre area is one of the most beautiful of the royal parks and dates back to the 16C. It was remodelled by John Nash (1829) who created the lake now full of pelicans and numerous varieties of waterfowl. To the north of the park is **The Mall**★★, the processional way from Buckingham Palace to Whitehall.

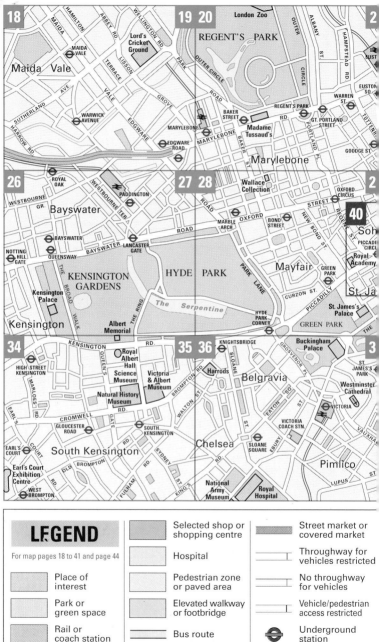

LEGEND

For map pages 18 to 41 and page 44

Place of interest	Selected shop or shopping centre
Park or green space	Hospital
Rail or coach station	Pedestrian zone or paved area
	Elevated walkway or footbridge
	Bus route
	Street market or covered market
	Throughway for vehicles restricted
	No throughway for vehicles
	Vehicle/pedestrian access restricted
	Underground station

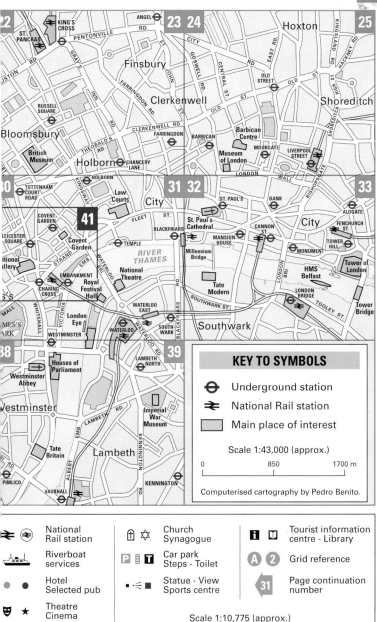

22 ST. PANCRAS KING'S CROSS PENTONVILLE RD. GRAY'S INN RD. EUSTON RD.

ANGEL 23 24 Hoxton 25 KINGSLAND RD. HACKNEY RD.

CITY RD. PENTONVILLE RD.

Finsbury

FARRINGDON RD. JOHN ST. GOSWELL RD. CENTRAL ST. EAST RD. OLD STREET OLD ST. SHOREDITCH HIGH ST. KINGSLAND RD.

Clerkenwell

Shoreditch

Bloomsbury

British Museum

THEOBALD'S RD. CLERKENWELL RD. FARRINGDON

Holborn CHANCERY LANE

Barbican BARBICAN Barbican Centre MOORGATE LIVERPOOL STREET BISHOPSGATE

Museum of London LONDON WALL

30 TOTTENHAM COURT ROAD HOLBORN KINGSWAY

Law Courts City 31 32 ST. PAUL'S BANK 33 ALDGATE

FLEET ST. St. Paul's Cathedral City FENCHURCH ST.

LEICESTER SQUARE COVENT GARDEN Covent Garden BLACKFRIARS CANNON ST. TOWER HILL

ational llery STRAND TEMPLE RIVER THAMES Millennium Bridge MANSION HOUSE MONUMENT LONDON BRI. Tower of London

EMBANKMENT CHARING CROSS Royal Festival Hall National Theatre Tate Modern HMS Belfast LONDON BRIDGE TOOLEY ST. Tower Bridge

WATERLOO EAST SOUTHWARK ST. BLACKFRIARS RD.

MES'S ARK WHITEHALL VICTORIA EMB. London Eye WATERLOO WESTMINSTER SOUTH WARK Southwark

38 Houses of Parliament WATERLOO RD. LAMBETH NORTH 39

Westminster Abbey

Westminster LAMBETH RD. EMB. Imperial War Museum KENNINGTON RD.

Tate Britain ALBERT Lambeth

PIMLICO

VAUXHALL KENNINGTON

KEY TO SYMBOLS

⊖ Underground station

⇌ National Rail station

▢ Main place of interest

Scale 1:43,000 (approx.)

0   850   1700 m

Computerised cartography by Pedro Benito.

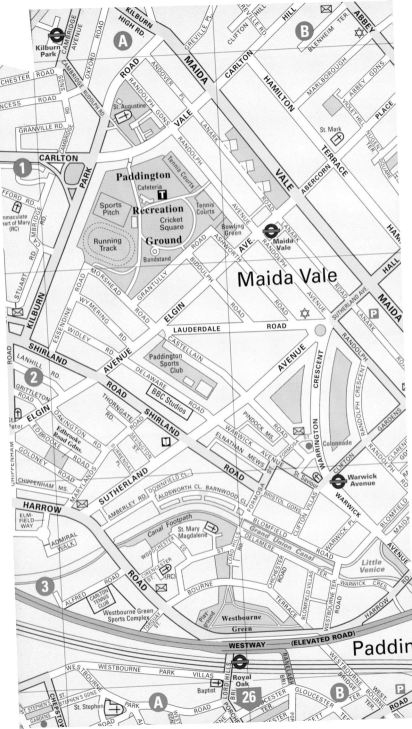

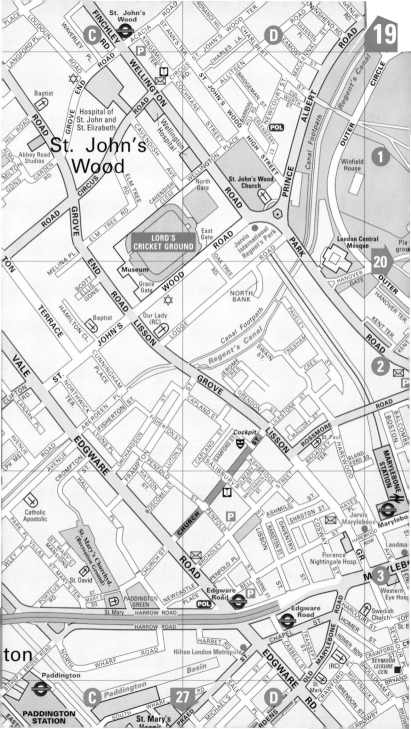

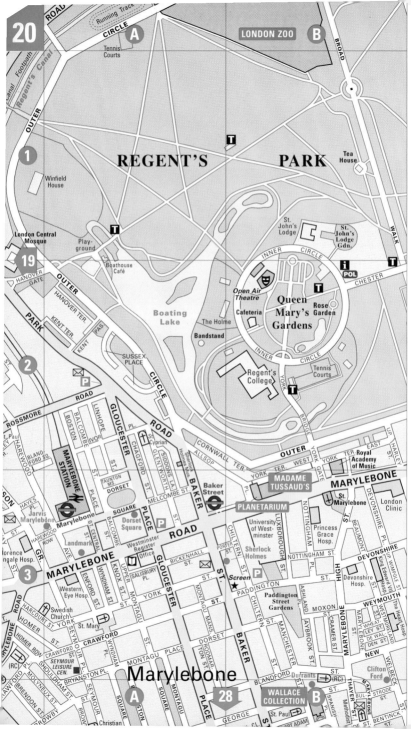

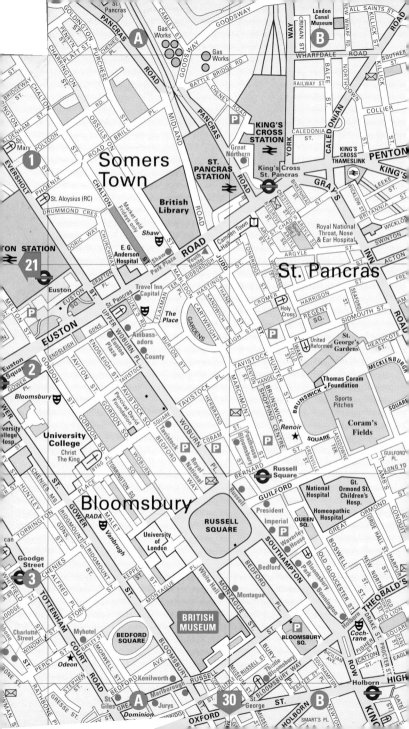

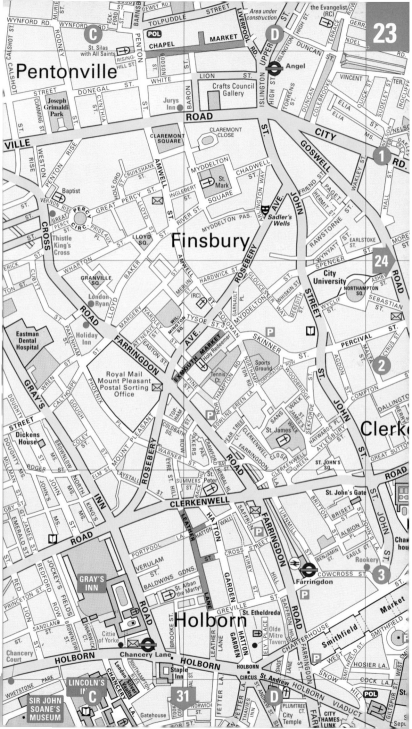

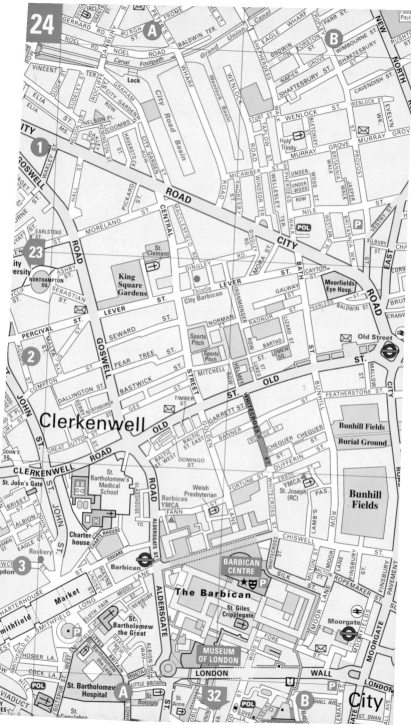

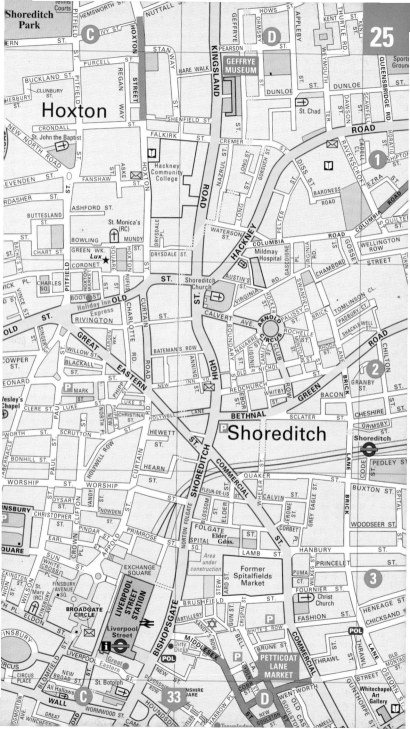

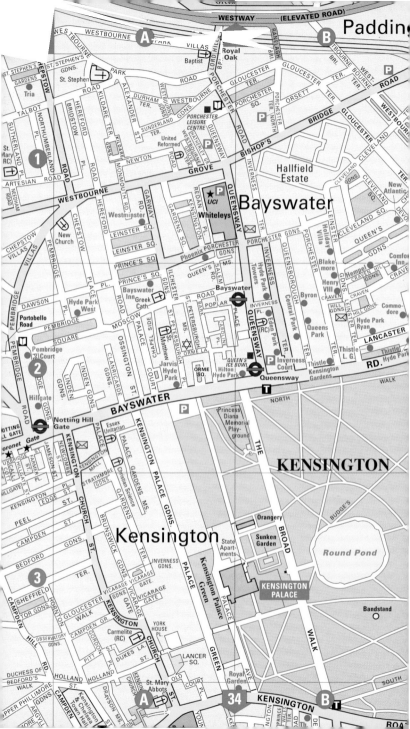

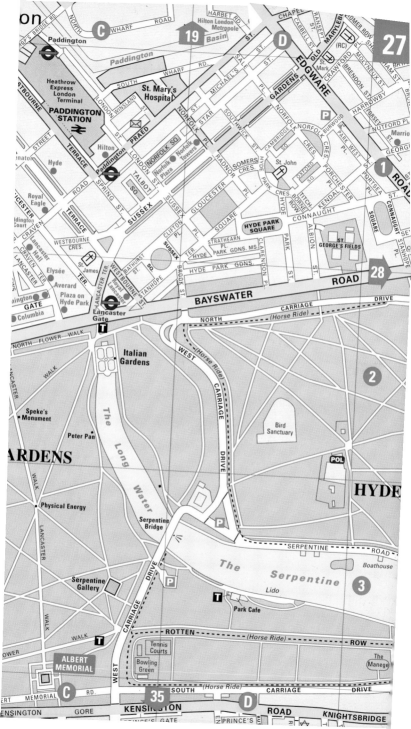

on

C WHARF ROAD

HARBET RD.

Hilton London
Metropole

19 Basin

CHAPEL

CABELL ST.

RANSEY

D OLD

MARYLEB

ROMER ROW

HAM ST.

BRY

EDGWARE

Paddington

Paddington

SOUTH WHARF RD.

Heathrow
Express
London
Terminal

**PADDINGTON
STATION**

St. Mary's
Hospital

MICHAEL'S PL.

SALE ST.

GARDENS

St.
Mark
(RC)

BRENDON ST.

MOLYNEUX ST.

CRAWFORD

HARROWBY

NUTFORD PL.

WESTBOURNE

STREET

LONDON ST.

WINSLAND ST.

PRAED

NORFOLK SQ.

STAR ST.

SOUTHWICK ST.

CAMBRIDGE

NORFOLK

PORCHESTER

SQ.

NORFOLK CRES.

BURWOOD

PARK WEST PL.

NUTFORD PL.

Marrio

GEORG

Hilton

Paddington

Hyde

TERRACE

P

Norfolk
Plaza

Norfolk
Towers

TALBOT SQ.

SUSSEX

St John

SOMERS CRES.

HYDE PARK CRES.

OXFORD SQ.

BOWER

KENDAL ST.

PORCHESTER PL.

PORTSEA

SQUARE

CONNAUGHT

1

ROAD

Royal
Eagle

dington
Court

CRAVEN
HALL

Lancaster
Hall

Elysée

Averard

Plaza on
Hyde Park

Columbia

ngton
GATE

LANCASTER TER.

WESTBOURNE TER.

BATHURST ST.

STANHOPE TER.

WESTBOURNE CRES.

GLOUCESTER

SQUARE

SUSSEX

CLIFTON PL.

SUSSEX SQ.

**HYDE PARK
SQUARE**

STRATHEARN
PL.

HYDE PARK GDNS. MS.

HYDE PARK GDNS.

CLARENDON PL.

ALBION ST.

HYDE PARK ST.

**ST.
GEORGE'S FIELDS**

STANHOPE

CONNAUGHT

SQUARE

STANHOPE

28

St.
James

Royal
Lancaster

Lancaster
Gate

T

BROOK ST.

BAYSWATER

ROAD

NORTH

CARRIAGE

(Horse Ride)

DRIVE

NORTH — FLOWER — WALK

Italian
Gardens

WEST

(Horse Ride)

2

LANCASTER

WALK

Speke's
Monument

Peter Pan

RDENS

The
Long
Water

CARRIAGE

DRIVE

Bird
Sanctuary

POL

HYDE

Physical Energy

LANCASTER

WALK

Serpentine
Bridge

P

SERPENTINE

ROAD

Boathouse

Serpentine
Gallery

P

DRIVE

CARRIAGE

The

Serpentine

3

Lido

T

Park Cafe

WALK

T

ROTTEN

(Horse Ride)

ROW

**ALBERT
MEMORIAL**

Tennis
Courts

Bowling
Green

The
(Manege)

OWER

ERT

C

MEMORIAL RD.

WEST

CARRIAGE

35

SOUTH

(Horse Ride)

CARRIAGE

DRIVE

D

KENSINGTON

PRINCE'S GATE

EN

PRINCE'S

ROAD

KNIGHTSBRIDGE

GORE

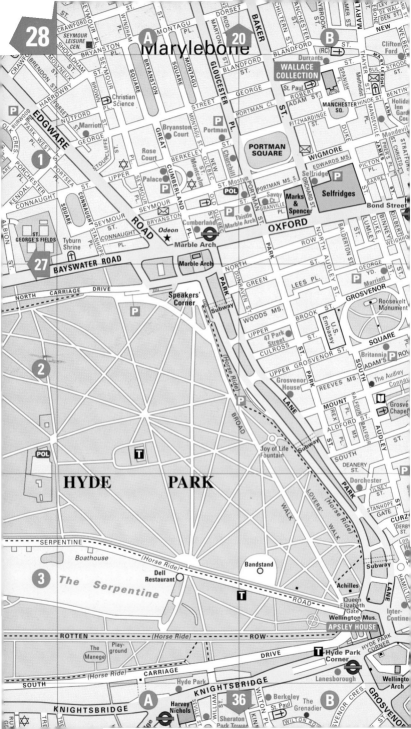

Marylebone

20

A   MONTAGU   ST.

B   ST.

SEYMOUR   ST.   DORSET   ST.   BAKER   CHILTERN   ST.   MANCHESTER   ST.   MARYLEBONE   NEW   WELBECK   ST.

CRAWFORD   WYNDHAM   ST.   MONTAGU   SQUARE   MARTON   ST.   ROD   BLANDFORD   ST.   Durrants   (RC)   Clifton   Ford   ST.   DE   WAL   DEN   ST.

SHOULDHAM   BRYANSTON   PL.   GLOUCESTER   BLANDFORD   ST.   WALLACE   COLLECTION   Methodist   THAYER   STRODE

SEYMOUR   LEISURE   CEN.   BRYANSTON   SQUARE   GEORGE   ST.   St. Paul   ROBERT   ADAM   SPANISH   Holiday   Inn   Garden   Ct   BENTIN

HARROWBY   Christian   Science   PORTMAN   CL.   ST.   FITZHARDINGE   MANCHESTER   SQ.   HINDE   ST.   MANDEVILLE   Mandevi

NUTFORD   Bryanston   Court   MONTAGU   STREET   GREAT   Portman   PORTMAN   SQUARE   DUKE   ST.   PICTON   ST.   BARRE   ST.   STRATFORD

EDGWARE   GEORGE   Marriott   STOURCLIFFE   Berkeley   NEW   Churchill   WIGMORE   EDWARDS MS   Selfridge   PICTON   BINNEY   CHRISTO

PORCHESTER   Rose   Court   UPPER   BERKELEY   Montcalm   Selfridge   DUKE   St.   P   Selfridges   Bond Street

KENDAL   CONNAUGHT   Palace   ST. MOSTYN   Savoy   Ct   PORTMAN MS. S.   Marks   &   Spencer   BALDERTON ST.   UMLEY   WEIGHO   GILBERT   ST.

ALBION   SEYMOUR   CONNAUGHT   STANHOPE   PL.   BRYANSTON   Cumberland   POL   Thistle   Marble Arch   Granville   PL.   OXFORD   NORTH   GEORGE   YD.   Marriott   P   ROW

ST.   GEORGE'S FIELDS   CONNAUGHT   ROAD   Odeon   ★   Marble Arch   Marble Arch   NORTH   ROW   AUDLEY   LEES PL.   GROSVENOR   The Audley   Connaught   Roosevelt   Monument

27   BAYSWATER ROAD   Tyburn   Shrine   Marble Arch   NORTH   DUNRAVEN   GREEN   ST.   BROOK   U.S.   Embassy   SQUARE   Britannia   P   ROW

NORTH   CARRIAGE   DRIVE   Speakers'   Corner   Subway   WOODS MS.   47 Park   Street   UPPER   GROSVENOR   ST.   REEVES MS.   ADAM'S   PL.

P   CULROSS   ST.   Grosvenor   House   MOUNT   ST.   Grosve   Chapel

2   PARK   LANE   (Horse Ride)   BROAD   Joy of Life   Fountain   Subway   MOUNT   ST.   BALFOUR   ST.   AUDLEY   ST.

POL   T   HYDE   PARK   WALK   SOUTH   ST.   DEANERY   Dorchester   P   STANHOPE   CURZ

SERPENTINE   (Horse Ride)   LOVERS'   Subway   TILNEY   ST.   GATE   DERBY   Lon   ST.

Boathouse   Bandstand   WALK   (Horse Ride)

3   The   Serpentine   Dell   Restaurant   T   ROAD   Achilles   Queen   Elizabeth   Gate   Wellington Mus.   APSLEY HOUSE   Inter-   Contine

ROTTEN   (Horse Ride)   ROW   DRIVE   T   Hyde Park   Corner   Lanesborough   HYDE PARK   CORNER   Wellingto   Arch

The   Manege   ground   CARRIAGE   Hyde Park   Lanesborough   GROSVENOR   CRES.

SOUTH   (Horse Ride)   A   KNIGHTSBRIDGE   36   WILTON   B   GROSVENO

KNIGHTSBRIDGE   Harvey   Nichols   SLOANE   WILLIAM   ST.   St. Paul   Berkeley   The   Grenadier   WILTON ROW   KIN

Sheraton   Park Tower

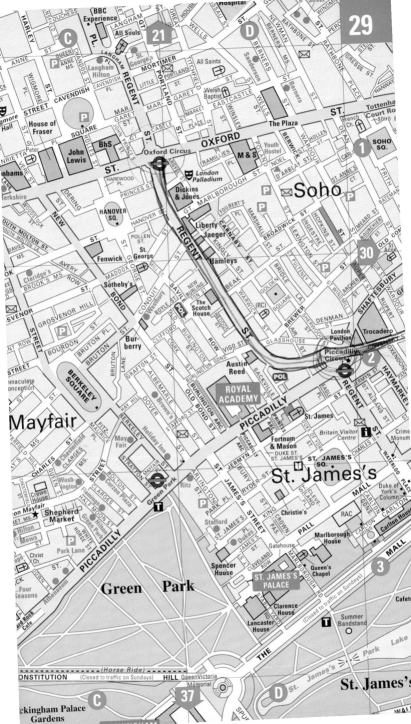

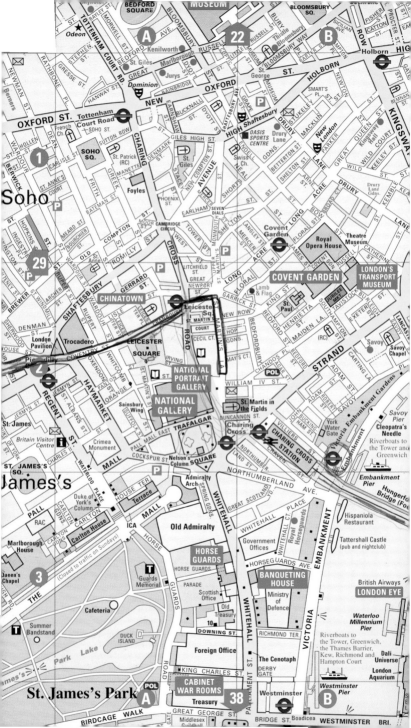

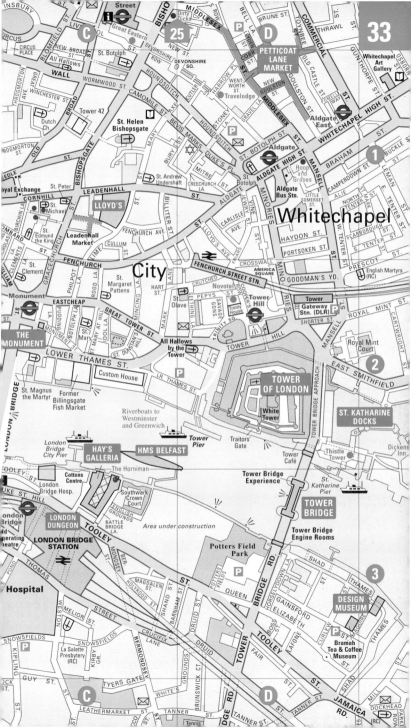

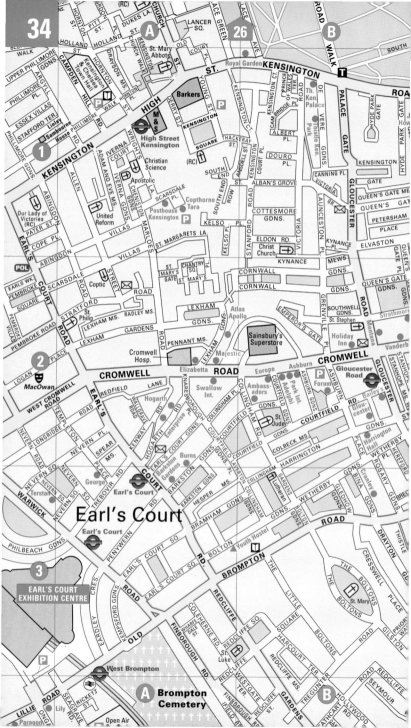

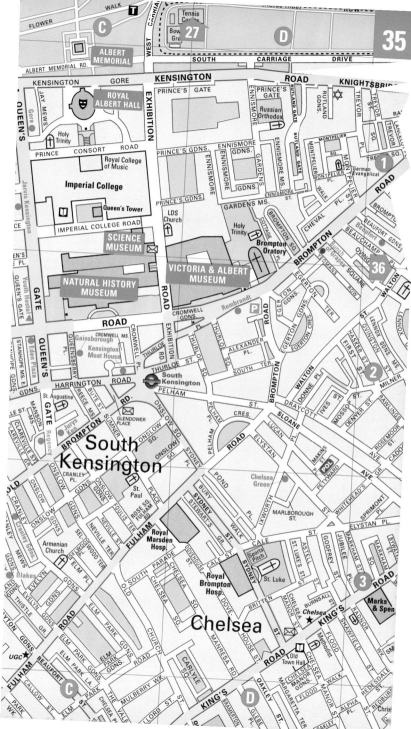

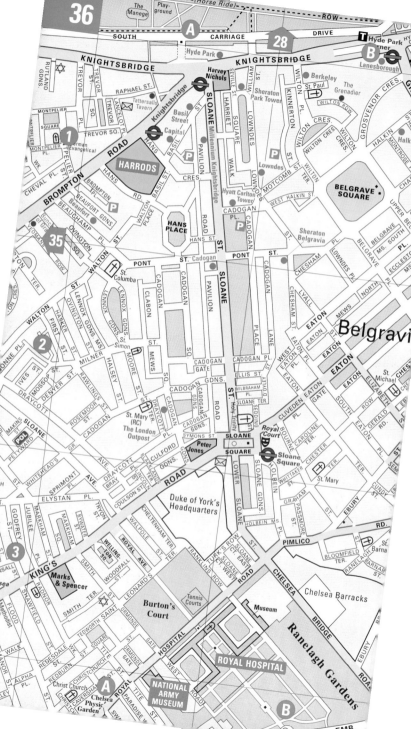

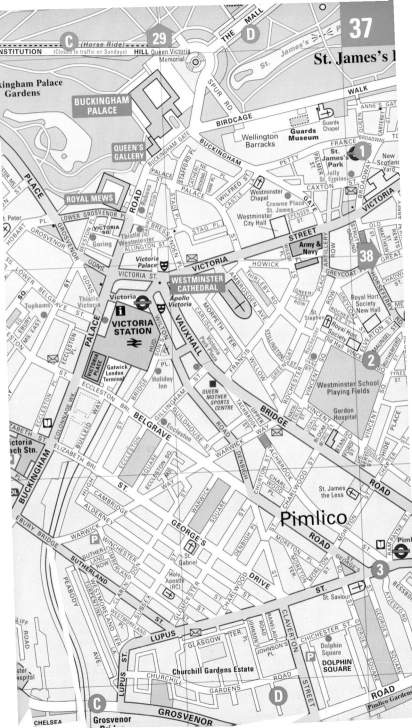

C (Horse Ride) 29
NSTITUTION (Closed to traffic on Sundays) HILL Queen Victoria
Memorial

THE MALL D

St. James's

kingham Palace
Gardens

WALK

BUCKINGHAM PALACE

BIRDCAGE

ANNE'S GATE

Wellington
Barracks

Guards
Museum

Guards
Chapel

BROADWAY

FRANCE

QUEEN'S GALLERY

BUCKINGHAM

PETTY

PALMER ST.

St.
James's
Park

Jolly
St. Ermins

1

New
Scotland
Yard

ROYAL MEWS

STAFFORD PL.

CATHERINE PL.

BUCKING. PL.

WILFRED ST.

CASTLE LA.

Westminster
Chapel

Crowne Plaza
St. James

CAXTON

VICTORIA

ROAD

Tothills

PALACE

STAG PL.

BRESSENDEN PL.

STAG PL.

SPENSER
ST.

Westminster
City Hall

STREET

OLD

MATHEW

ARTILLERY

GREAT

t. Peter

LOWER GROSVENOR PL.

GROSVENOR PL.

VICTORIA SQ.

Goring

ALLINGTON ST.

Victoria
Palace

VICTORIA

HOWICK

Army & Navy

PLACE

ROW

GREYCOAT

CHADWI

38

GREAT

Thistle
Westminster

THIRLEBY RD.

GREEN-
COAT
ROW

Royal Hort.
Society
New Hall

HORSEFERR

ME

Tophams

Thistle
Victoria

Victoria

WESTMINSTER CATHEDRAL

Apollo
Victoria

AMBROSDEN AVE.

MORPETH TER.

St.
Stephen

Royal Hort.
Society
Old Hall

ROCHESTER

VINCENT

2

VICTORIA STATION

VAUXHALL

CARLISLE PL.

Victoria
Park Plaza

STILLINGTON ST.

GREENCOAT

VAN.
ST.

SQ.

Westminster School
Playing Fields

FYNES
ST.

VICTORIA PLACE

Gatwick
London
Terminal

PL.

Holiday
Inn

FRANCIS

ST.

WILLOW

ROCHESTER

ST.

NATH.

Gordon
Hospital

VINCENT

STAN.

DOUGLAS

CHIDE

PLACE

ctoria
ach Stn.

ECCLESTON

BRIDGE

BELGRAVE

GUILDHOUSE ST.

Eccleston

ROAD

TACHBROOK ST.

UPPER

BRIDGE

VINCENT

BLOOM.

VINCENT

ROAD

St. James
the Less

ELIZABETH BRI.

ECCLESTON

SQUARE

WARWICK

DENBIGH

CHURTON

CHARLWOOD

PL.

BUCKINGHAM

HUGH

CAMBRIDGE

ALDERNEY

ST.

ECCLESTON

SQUARE

WAY

GEORGE'S

WARWICK

SQUARE

ST.

DENBIGH

MORETON

MORETON

PL.

MORETON

TER.

MORETON

SO.

ROAD

RAM. PAYNE ST.

Pimlico

Piml

3

EBURY BRIDGE

WARWICK

P

WINCHESTER

SUTHER-
LAND

CUMBERLAND

ROW

SUTHERLAND

WESTMORELAND

TURRENTINE

St.
Gabriel

Holy
Apostle
(RC)

CHARLWOOD

ST.

GLOUCESTER

ST.

DRIVE

CHARLWOOD

ST.

ST.

St. Saviour

CHICHESTER ST.

GEORGE'S

GEORGE'S

SQUARE

AYLESFORD

BESSBOR

LIFF

ROAD

PEABODY

SUTHERLAND

WESTMORELAND TER.

LUPUS

ST.

ESSEX ST.

JOHNSON'S PL.

JOHNSON'S
PL.

GLASGOW TER.

Dolphin
Square

DOLPHIN SQUARE

P

ster
ospital

LUPUS

ST.

CHURCHILL

Churchill Gardens Estate

GARDENS

RANELAGH

ROAD

CLAVERTON

ROAD

STREET

ROAD

Pimlico Gardens

CHELSEA

C
Grosvenor

GROSVENOR

D

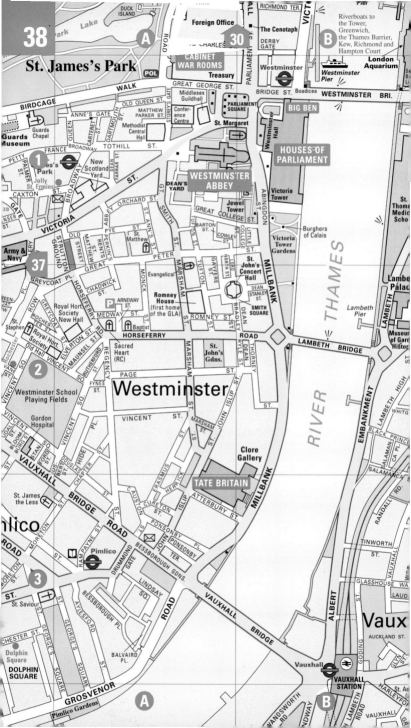

DUCK ISLAND

Foreign Office

The Cenotaph

RICHMOND TER.

Riverboats to
the Tower,
Greenwich,
the Thames Barrier,
Kew, Richmond and
Hampton Court

ST. CHARLES

DERBY
GATE

A

30

B

London
Aquarium

CABINET
WAR
ROOMS

Westminster

Treasury

Westminster
Pier

St. James's Park

POL

BRIDGE ST. Boadicea

WESTMINSTER BRI.

BIRDCAGE

WALK

OLD QUEEN ST.

GREAT GEORGE ST.

Middlesex
Guildhall

STOREY'S GATE

Conference
Centre

PARLIAMENT
SQUARE

BIG BEN

ANNE'S GATE

MATTHEW
PARKER ST.

Methodist
Central
Hall

St. Margaret

Westminster
Hall

Guards Chapel

Guards
Museum

DARTMOUTH

QUEEN

CARTERET

Westminster
Hall

WESTMINSTER ABBEY

HOUSES OF PARLIAMENT

PETTY
FRANCE

1

es's
Park

New Scotland Yard

BROADWAY

TOTHILL ST.

DEAN'S
YARD

ABINGDON ST.

Victoria
Tower

PALMER
ST.

Jolly
St. Ermins

CAXTON
GATE

VICTORIA

OLD

ORCHARD

ST.

ST. ANN'S ST.

GREAT

COLLEGE ST.

Jewel
Tower

St.
Thomas
Medic
Scho

Victoria
Tower

BROADWAY

ABB

PYE

PERKINS'

BARTON ST.

COWLEY ST.

LITTLE

Burghers
of Calais

37

Army &
Navy

STRUTTON
GROUND

ST. MATTHEW

RENTS'

St.
Matthew

PETER

MONCK

GREAT

MARSHAM

TUFTON

GAYFERE ST.

NORTH ST.

DEAN

St.
John's
Concert
Hall

Victoria
Tower
Gardens

Lambeth
Pier

Lambe
Pala

St.
Stephen

Royal Hort.
Society
New Hall

P

ARNEWAY
ST.

CHADWICK
ST.

MEDWAY

Romney
House
(first home
of the GLA)

ROMNEY ST.

DEAN
STANLEY
ST.

SMITH
SQUARE

Museum
of Gard
Histor

Rochester

ELVERTON

Royal Hort.
Society
Old Hall

VINCENT

Baptist

HORSEFERRY

MAUNSEL
ST.

ROAD

LAMBETH BRIDGE

2

VAN

SO.

RUTHERFORD

REGENCY

Sacred
Heart
(RC)

PAGE

St. John's
Gdns.

RYLE ST.

THORNEY

DEAN

VINCENT

FYNES
ST.

Westminster

THAMES

Westminster School
Playing Fields

VINCENT

Gordon
Hospital

VINCENT

ST.

PL.

DOUGLAS

MARSHAM ST.

JOHN ISLIP

VINCENT

ST.

RIVER

VAUXHALL

STAN.
SO.

HIDE

CHAPTER

ST. JAMES
the Less

BRIDGE

ROAD

RASMUS

HERRICK

Clore
Gallery

MILLBANK

EMBANKMENT

LAMBETH HIGH

WHITG

BLACK PRINCE

RANDALI

SALAMANCA

CA PL.

SALAMANCA ST.

lico

ST.

MORETON

RAMPAYNE ST.

CAUSTON

CURETON
ST.

ISLIP

ATTERBURY ST.

TATE BRITAIN

SALAMANCA

3

St. Saviour

Pimlico

DRUMMOND
GATE

BESSBOROUGH GDNS.

PONSONBY

JOHN

TER.

PONSONBY
PL.

TINWORTH

ST.

GLASSHOUSE WA

LAUD

Dolphin
Square

AYLESFORD

BESSBOROUGH
PL.

LINDSAY
SQ.

Vaux

AUCKLAND ST.

**DOLPHIN
SQUARE**

CHESTER ST.

ST. GEORGE'S

GEORGE'S

SQUARE

BALVAIRD
PL.

VAUXHALL

BRIDGE

ROAD

GODING

Vauxhall

**VAUXHALL
STATION**

LAMBETH

HARLEYFO

Pimlico Gardens

A

GROSVENOR

B

WANDSWORTH

NDWAY

VAUXHALL

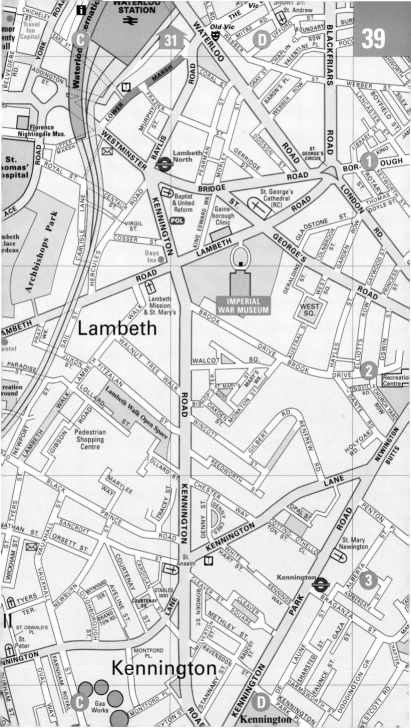

WATERLOO STATION

CHICHELEY ROAD
ST. Travel Inn Capital
BELVEDERE RD.
YORK ROAD
LAKE ST.
ADDINGTON ST.

THE Vic
Old Vic
St. Andrew
SHORT ST.
MITRE RD.
UFFORD
BLACKFRIARS
SURR

WATERLOO ROAD
WEBBER ROW
BOUNDARY ROW
POCC
SILEX ST.
BOYFIELD
LANCASTER ST.

MARSH
CORAL ST.
GRAY'S
BARON'S PL.
WEBBER ROW
CHAPLIN ST.
VALENTINE PL.

Florence Nightingale Mus.
FRAZIER ST.
MURPHY ST.

WESTMINSTER BRIDGE ROAD
LOWER MARSH
UPPER MARSH
ROYAL ST.
CENTAUR ST.
BAYLIS
Lambeth North
PEARMAN ST.
MORLEY ST.
GERRIDGE ST.
DODSON ST.
ST. GEORGE'S CIRCUS
LIBRARY ST.
KING
ROTARY
KEYWORTH ST.
THOMAS ST.
DOYLE ST.
BOR-OUGH
1

St.
homas'
ospital
St. Thomas' Hospital

Archbishops Park
CARLISLE LANE
HERCULES ROAD
VIRGIL ST.
COSSER ST.
Days Inn

Baptist & United Reform
POL
KING EDWARD WK.
Gainsborough Clinic
St. George's Cathedral (RC)
LONDON RD.
GLADSTONE ST.
COLNBROOK ST.
GARDEN ROW
GAYWOOD ST.
PRINCESS ST.

Lambeth Palace Gardens

LAMBETH ROAD
KENNINGTON ROAD
ST. GEORGE'S ROAD
GERALDINE ST.
WEST SQ.
WEST SQ.

Lambeth

Lambeth Mission & St. Mary's
WALK
PRATT WK.
SAIL ST.
JUXON ST.
LAMBETH WALK
FITZALAN ST.
LOLLARD ST.
Lambeth Walk Open Space
WALNUT TREE WALK
WALCOT SQ.
ST. MARY'S GDNS
ST. MARY'S WK.
MONKTON ST.
BROOK DRIVE
BROOK DRIVE
AUSTRAL ST.
HAYES
ELLIOTTS ROW
OSWIN ST.
DRIVE
2
Recreation Centre

IMPERIAL WAR MUSEUM

LONGVILLE RD.
DANTE RD.
CHURCH YARD ROW
HOLYOAK RD.

wotel
PARADISE ST.
reation round
NEWPORT ST.
GIBSON ROAD
LAMBETH WALK
LOLLARD ST.
Pedestrian Shopping Centre
BISHOP GARDEN
WINCOTT ST.
REEDWORTH ST.
GILBERT RD.
RENFREW RD.
NEWINGTON BUTTS

BLACK PRINCE ROAD
MARYLEE WAY
SANCROFT ST.
ORSETT ST.
TRACEY ST.
KENNINGTON ROAD
CHESTER WAY
DENNY ST.
DENNY CRES.
KENNINGTON LANE
PENTON PL.

St. Anselm
WHITE HART ST.
OPAL ST.
COTTINGTON ST.
OTHELLO CL.
St. Mary Newington
KENNINGTON ROAD
ALBERTA ST.
AMBERGATE ST.
3

WICKHAM ST.
NATHAN ST.
VAUXHALL ST.
TYERS ST.
TYERS TER.
ST. OSWALD'S PL.
St. Peter
NEWBURN ST.
LOUGHBOROUGH
WYNYARD TER.
BRANDON RD.
AVELINE ST.
COURTENAY
COURTENAY SQ.
CARDIGAN ST.
STABLES WAY
KENNINGTON LANE
CLEAVER ST.
BOWDEN ST.
CLEAVER SQUARE
METHLEY ST.
Kennington
KENNINGTON PARK
KENNINGTON ROAD
KENNINGS WAY
BRAGANZA ST.
GAZA ST.
LAUNE ST.
SHARSTED ST.
FAUNCE ST.
HARMSWORTH ST.
DE LAUNE ST.
CHAPTER

Kennington
MONTFORD PL.
MILVERTON ST.
RAVENSDON ST.
RADCOT ST.
STANNARY ST.
KENNINGTON PARK RD.
KENNINGTON
Kennington

OVAL WAY
FARNHAM ROYAL
Gas Works
MONTFORD PL.
D
KENNINGTON
DODDINGTON GR.
WESTCOTT RD.

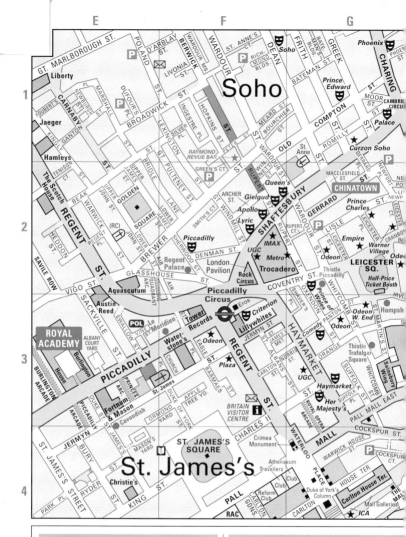

TIPS FOR THEATREGOERS

Details and times of theatre performances are given in the quality daily newspapers, while more comprehensive information can be found in weekly magazines such as *Time Out* and *What's On* on sale at news-vendors. There is also a free fortnightly *London Theatre Guide* available from theatres, hotels and tourist information centres throughout central London.

Some tickets for same day performances are available for just over half price on the south side of Leicester Square at the **Half-Price Ticket Booth** (see map square G2 above). *The booth is open Mon-Sat noon-6.30pm, Sun noon-3pm; cash purchases only; early queuing is advisable.*

MAIN THEATRES & CONCERT HALLS

Adelphi	41 J2	Duchess	41 K:
Albery	41 H2	Duke of York's	41 H:
Aldwych	41 K1	Fortune	41 K
Apollo	40 F2	Garrick	41 H:
Apollo Victoria	37 C2	Gielgud	40 F:
Barbican Hall	24 B3	Haymarket	40 G:
Barbican Theatre	24 B3	Her Majesty's	40 G:
Cambridge	41 H1	London Palladium	29 D:
Coliseum	41 H3	Lyceum	41 K:
Comedy	40 G3	Lyric	40 F:
Criterion	40 F3	National Theatre	31 C
Dominion	30 A1	- Cottesloe	
Donmar Warehouse	41 H1	- Lyttelton	
Drury Lane	41 K1	- Olivier	

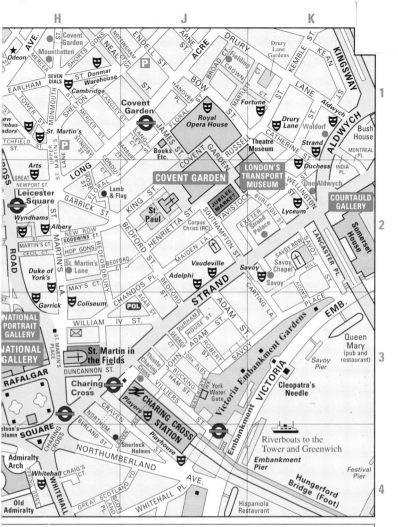

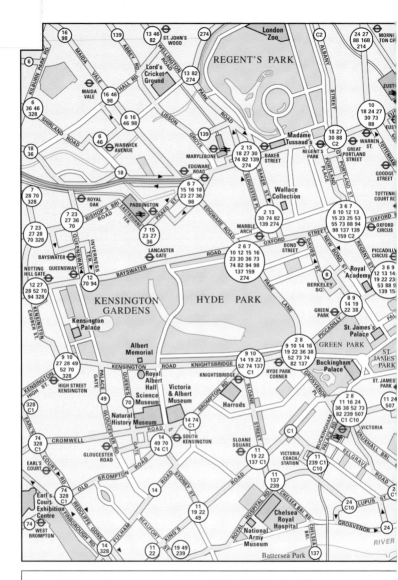

Travel Information

London Transport Travel Information Centres provide free Underground, bus and rail maps. You will find these centres in the Underground stations at Heathrow Airport (Terminals 1, 2, 3), Oxford Circus, Piccadilly Circus, St. James's Park, King's Cross and Liverpool Street; also at Victoria and Euston main line rail stations and at Heathrow Airport Arrivals in Terminals 1, 2 and 4. For full travel details call 020-7222 1234 or visit www.transportforlondon.gov.uk.

The Underground

Also known as the "Tube", this is the fastest way to travel around London, especially over long distances. To help plan your journey use the Underground Map *(see back cover of this publication)* which has been designed to indicate clearly which stations allow you to transfer from one line to another. The Underground system is divided into six fare zones, with the city centre being in Zone 1. The price of a ticket depends on how many zones you travel through.

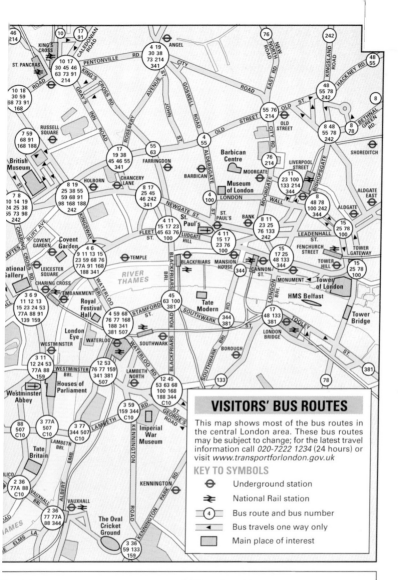

VISITORS' BUS ROUTES

This map shows most of the bus routes in the central London area. These bus routes may be subject to change; for the latest travel information call *020-7222 1234* (24 hours) or visit *www.transportforlondon.gov.uk*

KEY TO SYMBOLS

⊖	Underground station
⇌	National Rail station
④	Bus route and bus number
◄	Bus travels one way only
▢	Main place of interest

Buses

Most buses are red double-deckers. There are two types of stop: *compulsory* (sign with white background) where all buses indicated will stop without being hailed, unless they are full; *request* (sign with red background) where buses stop only when you raise your hand allowing the driver to see you well in advance. Bus fares vary according to whether or not the journey is wholly outside Zone 1 or passes through Zone 1.

Travelcards

There are various types of Travelcard (One Day, Seven Day, Weekend, Family and LT Card) which give virtually unlimited travel within the zones you choose on the buses, Underground, Docklands Light Railway, Tramlink and most National Rail services in the London zonal area *(excepting LT Cards)*. Available at Underground stations, Railway stations in the London area, Travel Information Centres, tourist information centres and at selected newsagents.

GREENWICH & ISLE OF DOGS

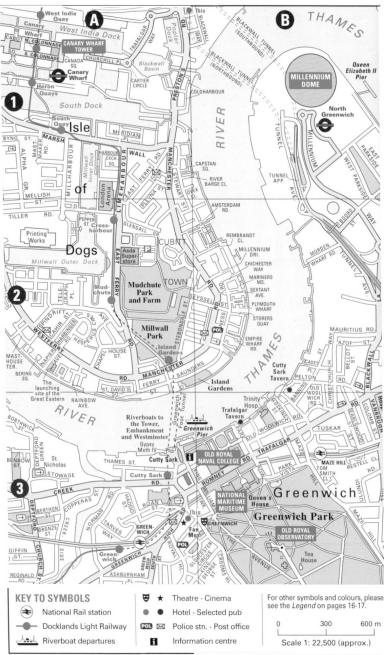

KEY TO SYMBOLS

- National Rail station
- Docklands Light Railway
- Riverboat departures
- Theatre - Cinema
- Hotel - Selected pub
- Police stn. - Post office
- Information centre

For other symbols and colours, please see the *Legend* on pages 16-17.

0   300   600 m

Scale 1: 22,500 (approx.)

INDEX TO STREETS

ABBREVIATIONS

		Cl.	-Close	Gt.	-Great	Pde.	-Parade	Ter.	-Terrace
App.	-Approach	Ct.	-Court	Gr.	-Grove	Pk.	-Park	Up.	-Upper
Arc.	-Arcade	Cres.	-Crescent	La.	-Lane	Pas.	-Passage	Vw.	-View
Ave.	-Avenue	Dri.	-Drive	Mkt.	-Market	Pl.	-Place	Vs.	-Villas
Blds.	-Buildings	E.	-East	Ms.	-Mews	Rd.	-Road	Wk.	-Walk
Bri.	-Bridge	Emb.	-Embankment	N.	-North	S.	-South	W.	-West
		Gdns.	-Gardens	Pal.	-Palace	Sq.	-Square	Yd.	-Yard

This index only comprises selected streets from map pages 18-39 inclusive.

45